Creative Garden Settings

John D. Webersinn
G. Daniel Keen

TAB BOOKS
Blue Ridge Summit, PA

FIRST EDITION
FIRST PRINTING

Note from the Authors:

Although every effort was made to make the plans and information in this book accurate, the possibility of error still exists. Consequently, double check plans completely before starting. The authors are not responsible for injury, damage, or loss, however caused, arising from the use of the information contained herein. Follow all safety precautions when working with hand and power tools. Check to see that all power tools are undamaged and in proper working order.

To more clearly describe the information in this book, trade names of some products are used. In no way is this an endorsement of any product nor is it a criticism of similar products not named.

Use common sense and make safety the first consideration and your projects will reward you with years of satisfaction.

Library of Congress Cataloging-in-Publication Data

Webersinn, John D.
    Creative garden settings / by John D. Webersinn and G. Daniel
Keen.
        p. cm.
    Includes index.
    ISBN 0-8306-3943-8 (hard)   ISBN 0-8306-3942-X (paper)
    1. Garden structures. 2. Garden lighting. I. Keen, Dan.
II. Title.
TH4961.W43   1992
690'.89—dc20   92-2559
                                                          CIP

TAB Books offers software for sale. For information and a catalog, please contact TAB Software Department, Blue Ridge Summit, PA 17294-0850.

Acquisitions Editor: Kimberly Tabor
Book Editor: Lori Flaherty
Director of Production: Katherine G. Brown
Book Design: Jaclyn J. Boone
Illustrator: Carol Chapin   HT3

This book is dedicated to John's wife
Cherrill, daughter Jennifer, and his Mom
and Dad.

Contents

Acknowledgments

We wish to express a special thank you to our many friends and relatives who have persevered with us through this project.

Introduction

Well-designed and installed landscaping features can add measurable enjoyment and economic value to your home. Landscape features need not be elaborate to be enjoyable. Adhering to some of the simple guidelines presented here can help you enhance your yard or garden for your own enjoyment, but boost your property value. Doing the construction yourself will not only make projects more economical, but provide personal satisfaction and a sense of accomplishment.

Only basic carpentry skills, such as the use of simple hand tools and power tools, along with the ability to follow simple construction guidelines are required to complete the projects. Chapter 1 covers the basic skills and practical information necessary to design and construct outdoor living spaces that are perfect for your family and your home, and we strongly recommend that you read chapter 1 before going further.

This book identifies landscape features where they will best complement your yard. The term *landscape features* refers to items such as walkways, patios, decks, fences, walls, fountains, arbors, statues, and reflecting pools (ponds). These features can extend your living space, provide privacy, help to manage a difficult terrain, and make getting from point A to point B more pleasurable.

All the projects presented in this book can be incorporated into a single garden. Obviously, not everyone will want or need all of the projects. Careful attention to designing and planning will show what projects will work in your own yard.

Regardless of the project you choose, you must first have a clear understanding of your needs so that your project will complement your environment. A deck might be perfect for your friend's home, but your needs and your backyard might best be served by a patio. Because you and your family, as well as your site, are unique, only you can design the perfect solution.

It is best to design landscaping features for a specific use, much the way you would visualize and use a room in your home. You can create a plan that focuses on a certain project each year for a succession of years or just choose one for this year's "family fun project."

This book provides an awareness of landscape features, their use within a garden, and their construction. For example, we explain how a feature such as a patio can be used within a landscape and then cover the basic principles needed for construction. Some planting guidelines are suggested, but these guidelines are general because of geographic and climatic variations.

After doing one project, you might be encouraged to pursue additional projects. We hope that your hours of painstaking planning and careful construction yield years of enjoyment in your outdoor living spaces and a sense of pride in the ability to say **"I built it myself."**

1

Getting started

Before you begin any of the projects in this book, it is a good idea to be familiar with the tools you'll need, the different characteristics of lumber, fastener types, safety precautions, local building codes, and more.

Not all projects have a materials list. Many of the projects, such as constructing a concrete patio, contain simple mathematic formulas for figuring out the materials you'll need. For projects that have a materials list, be sure to modify it if you have modified the project to meet special requirements.

In order to be fully aware of the cost of a project, consult local sources for the items on the materials list. It is best to consult several sources, because prices can vary greatly.

Safe projects are no accident

No project should be undertaken without first considering safety. The following points are general rules to add to your "toolbox of common sense":

- Always use three-prong extension cords with grounding plugs when operating power tools.
- Do not use power tools while standing on damp ground or in water.
- Unplug tools before changing bits, blades, or sandpaper.

- Never use a power tool without secure footing.
- Always use safety guards provided on machinery.
- Keep tools and power cords clean and free of damage.
- Never wear loose or dangling clothing that could be snagged by moving parts, such as shafts and blades.
- Keep work area free of debris.
- Keep children from underfoot and out of the work area.
- Wear eye protection (goggles) when the potential exists for flying debris.

Rules and regulations

Before building any project, you need to be aware of the local building rules, regulations, and any requirements in your area. Your local building inspector can determine what, if any, permits will be needed. A 12-volt lawn lighting system, for example, might not require a permit but an underground reflecting pool lighting system might.

Rules and regulations are dictated by local policy. Laws that govern construction are set by uniform construction codes (UCC) at the state level and are adhered to, and supplemented by, local ordinances. Because local laws must be equal to, or more stringent than, state laws, you need only worry about satisfying local codes.

Construction codes are designed to protect the general public. For example, substandard construction of a deck or ramp could lead to a potential hazard in the future.

Handicap access

Construction codes for handicap access are usually geared to commercial construction. While homeowners are not usually bound by these building codes, complying with handicap codes might be advisable even though you do not foresee a need for it. The relaxed comfort that handicap access affords, such as gradual grades on ramps, overwide walkways, and flat transitional areas between ramp sections, can enhance your enjoyment of the landscape.

Lumber basics

It is important to understand the types of lumber available and the many fasteners used for assembly. Due to milling, the finished size of lumber will always be less than its nominal size. Nominal size is the name given to the lumber's size, even though it might not be completely accurate. A 2×4 is a good example. A 2×4's actual finished working size is $1^1/2 \times 3^1/2$. Figure 1-1 represents other common dimensional lumbers.

Nominal	Actual
1 x 4	3/4" x 3 3/4"
1 x 6	3/4" x 5 3/4"
2 x 4	1 1/2" x 3 1/2"
2 x 6	1 1/2" x 5 1/2"
2 x 8	1 1/2" x 7 1/4"
2 x 10	1 1/2" x 9 1/4"
2 x 12	1 1/2" x 11 1/4"
4 x 4	3 1/2" x 3 1/2"
6 x 6	5 1/2" x 5 1/2"

Fig. 1-1. Representative dimensional lumber.

Lumber used to build any outdoor project should be highly resistant to rot and insect damage. Two naturally resistant woods are cedar and redwood heartwood. Pressure-treated lumber is your best choice for processed lumber. If wood types other than these are used, a sealer-preservative must be applied to supply the necessary resistance.

Pressure-treated lumber has a chemical preservative. The most common chemical preservative is chromated copper arsenate, identified on the label by the letters CCA. This preservative usually leaves the wood a greenish color, which fades with time and exposure.

Pressure-treated lumber is rated by the amount of chemical preservative retained by the wood. The most common retention level for outdoor construction is .40. This level of retention is suitable for direct ground contact. Figure 1-2 illustrates a standard pressure-treated label. Typical higher levels of retention are 1.0 and 2.0, which are used for a greater degree of decay resistance (not commonly used by the home do-it-yourselfer).

The chemicals used in pressure-treated lumber are hazardous. Special precautions for avoiding contact with sawdust from pressure-treated wood include eye protection, a particle mask, long sleeves, and long pants. Never use pressure-treated scrap lumber in your fireplace or wood-burning stove.

Board foot

Some dealers sell lumber by the board foot. This term refers to a board with measurements (thickness × width × length) that equal 144 cubic

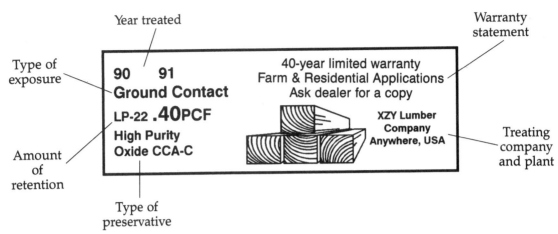

Year treated

Warranty statement

Type of exposure

90   91
Ground Contact

LP-22 **.40PCF**

**High Purity
Oxide CCA-C**

40-year limited warranty
Farm & Residential Applications
Ask dealer for a copy

**XZY Lumber
Company
Anywhere, USA**

Treating company and plant

Amount of retention

Type of preservative

Fig. 1-2. A typical label found on all pressure-treated lumber.

inches. This means that a board measuring $1'' \times 12'' \times 12''$ and also a board measuring $2'' \times 6'' \times 12''$ equals 144 cubic inches, or one board foot. Thickness times width times length divided by 12 equals board feet. You can determine the number of board feet in any given piece of lumber using this formula. For example, a $2 \times 4 \times 10'$ contains $6^{2}/3$ board feet:

$$2 \times 4 \times 10 = \frac{80}{12} = 6.6$$

Try to avoid lumber that is cupped, crooked, twisted, or bowed. These defects can cause headaches during construction. Be fussy. This way, you'll be able to get a finished project using the materials you determined to be the best for the grade used. For maximum strength, lumber should have a minimum of knots, cracks, or splits. Many lumber yards permit hand selection, as long as you don't leave a mess.

Fasteners

Just as wood needs to be treated to prevent decay, all fasteners should be of either a rustproof metal or galvanized to prevent rusting.

Nails

Figure 1-3 shows typical nail designations and associated sizes. Nails for outdoor projects should be resistant to rust. This is accomplished by the type of metal, such as aluminum, stainless steel, brass, or by a process of hot-dipped galvanizing.

Nails are sold by the penny length. The term *penny*, designated by

| Size | Length | Approx. # of Nails Per Pound | |
		Common	Finishing
2d	1"	850	
4d	1 1/2"	290	630
5d	1 3/4"	250	
6d	2"	160	290
8d	2 1/2"	100	195
10d	3"	65	125
12d	3 1/4"	60	
16d	3 1/2"	45	
20d	4"	30	

Fig. 1-3. Nail length and quantity in relation to its named size designation.

the letter d, the English abbreviation for penny, is a holdover from earlier days when nails were sold by the pound. Common sizes available are 8d, 10d, and 16d. A thousand nails 3 inches long weighing 10 pounds was given the designation 10 penny, or 10d. Likewise, 1,000 2-inch nails weighing 6 pounds were labeled 6 penny.

Nails longer than 20d, known in the trade as 20 penny, are usually referred to as spikes and are sold by their length (for example, a 12-inch spike).

Tools

Much of the tools and materials you'll need are basic to many of the projects in this book. A hammer, handsaw, carpenter's level, tape measure, framing square, line level, chalk line, screwdriver, chisel, plane, plumb bob, and wood file make up the basic hand tools needed. Some basic hand and power tools are shown in FIGS. 1-4 and 1-5. Power tools needed will include a drill, circular saw, and a saber saw. Some projects might require additional tools, such as a shovel, post hole digger, and a wheelbarrow, which will be identified with the project.

If you have more than a basic knowledge of power tools, you might choose to use a reciprocating saw or a pneumatic (air) tool to simplify jobs. A pneumatic nailer, for example, would make a large deck project quicker to assemble.

After reviewing all the basics of lumber, rules, and fasteners, it is time to concentrate on your proposed project.

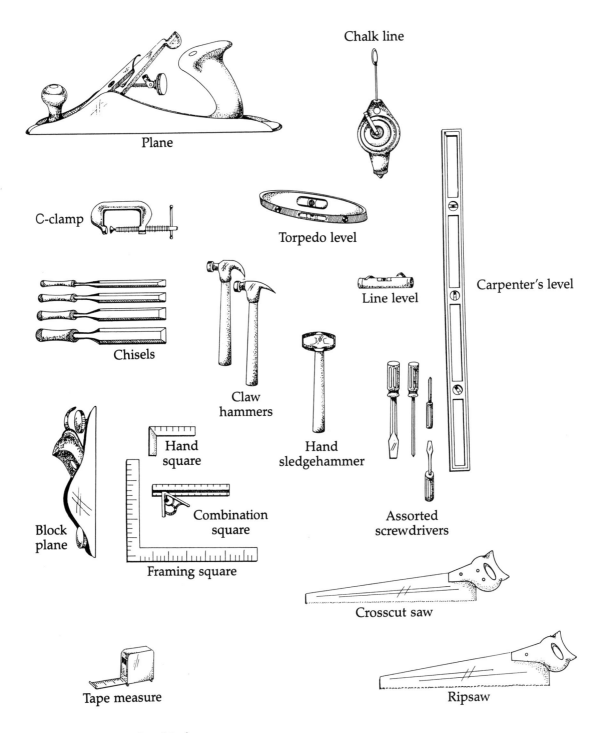

Plane

Chalk line

C-clamp

Torpedo level

Line level

Carpenter's level

Chisels

Claw
hammers

Hand
sledgehammer

Assorted
screwdrivers

Block
plane

Hand
square

Combination
square

Framing square

Crosscut saw

Tape measure

Ripsaw

Fig. 1-4. Common hand tools.

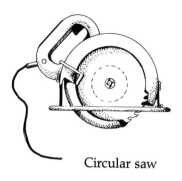

Circular saw

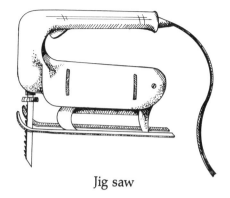

Jig saw

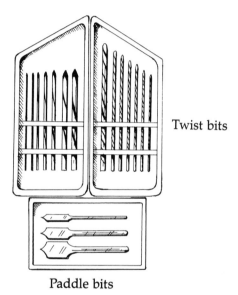

Twist bits

Paddle bits

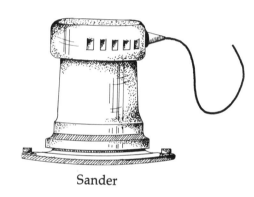

Sander

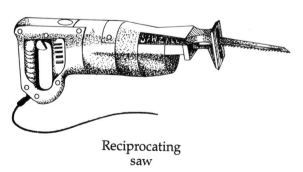

Reciprocating
saw

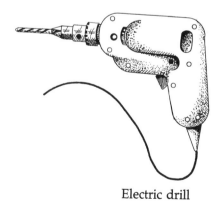

Electric drill

Fig. 1-5. Some recommended power tools.

Beginning a project

The thinking process of a project involves three phases: planning, reviewing, and installing. The first two phases are cyclic with each other. This means that you will repeat these steps until you arrive at a design that meets as many criteria as possible.

In phase one, walk around the proposed site. Get a clear idea of the views you will have of the project from many perspectives. As you see the proposed project from different angles, the design will start to mold itself. Seeing that a large, low specimen plant will crowd a deck, you might modify that space into a patio in order to get the full effect of both the surfaced area and the specimen plant.

Imagine, if you can, not only the views looking at the project but vistas that might be seen from the project. Views from within the house will also help solidify the design of your project. Resist the urge to rush into construction; spend time to develop the design. It is easier to correct mistakes in your design with pencil and eraser than with hammers and saws.

Good design is dictated by form and function. Integrate your project into your existing environment with as little disruption to the natural setting as possible. It might help to visualize the project more clearly if you "rough it out" with a garden hose or string line, marking the planned area clearly.

If you are considering an elevated space, you might find it helpful to stand on a ladder at different heights and at different locations to get a feel for the space. When you have done a complete survey of your property, you'll know intuitively what will work.

The second phase of project thinking involves reviewing your plan. At this point, the practical implementation of your "wish list" will become clear. The ideas presented in this book plus other projects you have seen and liked, will shape how the final project will be constructed.

The final phase, with the help of this book, is taking your project off the drafting board and constructing it in your yard.

2

Fences

Few man-made things have as much impact on the landscape as walls and fences. Except for an actual structure, no other element defines the character and function of the landscape as walls and fences do. From simple stone walls in farm fields (defining boundaries and ridding the land of obstructions for the plow) to elaborate wrought iron fences used purely for aesthetic reasons—walls and fences are an integral part of the landscape. There are picket fences for privacy, brick or wood fences to divide gardens, and seawalls or breakwaters to protect.

Historically, walls have been used to form a boundary to protect property from trespassers, shelter from wind and rain, provide privacy, and to retain soil and changes in grade. Fences, on the other hand, were originally intended to divide and protect properties but not shelter or provide privacy. The idea was that fences did not hide views and give privacy but rather helped to accentuate views.

Today, whether you plan on building a wall or a fence, it needs to fulfill the functions of your lifestyle, providing screening and privacy in certain areas and visual enhancement in others, as well as being aesthetically pleasing.

Fences can be used for many landscape purposes. A narrow property can be made to seem long and wide with the use of a low fence. If privacy is a concern, a fence constructed of wood or steel with green screens can help hide or intensify desirable features. A fence utilizing shade can help to modify the temperature a person experiences (see FIG. 2-1). Fences need not be only functional. They can also serve aesthetic

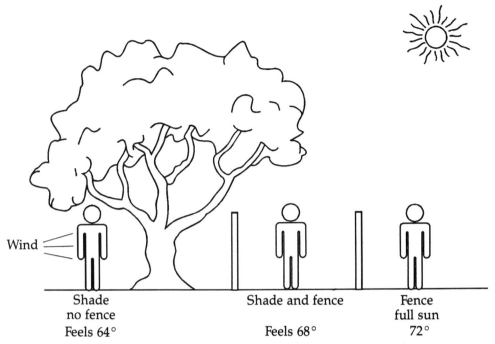

Wind

Shade
no fence
Feels 64°

Shade and fence
Feels 68°

Fence
full sun
72°

Fig. 2-1. The effects of shade and fences can have a dramatic impact on people.

needs. In this chapter, we'll identify several styles of fences and gates that can be used to enclose a garden space. The materials are as varied as the styles selected.

Restrictions

Before you begin erecting a fence, it is important to check local ordinances to see what restrictions might apply and where your property line is. Solid fences are oftentimes not permitted in situations that could create a hazard, such as near an intersection. Most local ordinances will also not permit a fence that positions the wrong side, or backside, of the fence toward your neighbor. The good side must face your neighbor.

Most ordinances will also not allow a fence taller than 6 feet along a property line. If more screening is desired, it might be possible to achieve this with a fence set inside the property line (FIG. 2-2). The location is determined by projecting a line at 45° toward your property and starting at the maximum allowable property line height. This should be done on a piece of graph paper.

Set up the graph with the Y axis equal to the fence height and the X axis equal to the distance from the property line. Referring to this graph would then show that you could install an 8-foot-high fence set 2 feet inside the property line or a 10-foot fence 4 feet inside the line (FIG. 2-3).

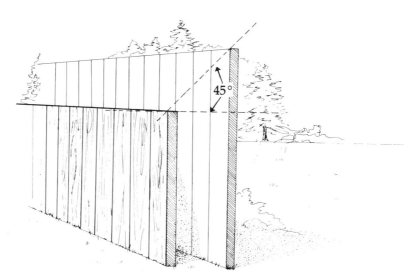

Fig. 2-2. *If you wish a fence higher than the legal limit, it might be possible using the 45-degree rule. Because most codes enforce the height of fences on property lines, moving the fence inside the property line can often solve the height problem.*

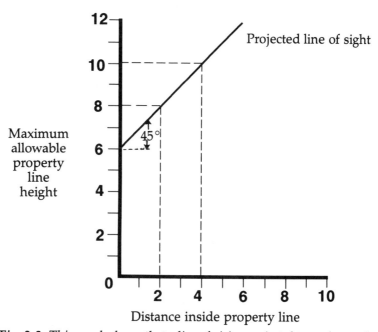

Fig. 2-3. *This graph shows that a line of vision projected towards your home and at a 45-degree angle provides for taller fences the farther in from the property line you locate your fence. In this case, at 2 feet inside the property line, an 8-foot-high fence might be allowed. Not all communities will allow this, so check carefully with local building officials.*

Check local ordinances to make sure this method is allowable in your community.

Design basics

It is always a good idea to plan any project first on paper. Corrections are easier to make with an eraser than with a hammer and saw. Using graph paper, sketch your home and property to an appropriate scale. Locate as accurately as possible any features that might affect, or be affected by,

Knee-High Plants

Botanical Name	Common Name
Buxus sempervirens	Boxwood
Ilex crenata Helleri	Helleri Holly
Rosa rugosa	Rugose Rose
Deutzia gracilis	Slender Deutzia
Azalea gumpo	Gumpo Azalea
Pieries japonica	Japanese Andromeda

Waist-High Plants

Botanical Name	Common Name
Taxus spp.	Yew
Berberis thunbergii	Barberry
Euonymus alatus compacta	Euonymus
Ilex crenata spp. and/or Ilex glabra	Holly
Spirea vanhouttei	Spirea
Juniperus chinensis glauca Hetzi	Juniper
Viburnum dentatum	Viburnum

Chest-High Plants

Botanical Name	Common Name
Thuja spp.	Arborvitae
Taxus cuspidata densiformis	Yew
Elaeagnus angustifolia	Russian Olive
Rhammus frangula Tallhedge	Tallhedge
Ligustrum ovalifolium	Privet
Syringa vulgaris	Lilac

Plants Eye-Level and Above

Botanical Name	Common Name
Pinus strobus	White Pine
Pseudotsuga menziesii	Douglas Fir
Tsuga candadensis	Canadian Hemlock
Picea pungens	Blue Spruce
Crataegus crusgalli	Hawthorn
Acer campestre	Hedge Maple

Fig. 2-4. Plants can be used as fences of varying heights, as seen in this partial list.

fencing. This would include driveways, walkways, patios, clotheslines, and gardens.

Lay a sheet of tracing paper on your sketch, using it as a base guide. This way, you can try out different ideas on individual sheets of tracing paper laid overtop of your base guide. Keep in mind that fences can be erected not only on the property line, but also within a garden to divide and define separate garden areas.

Your next step is to draw fences in areas where they are needed. Remember, plants make great fences when planted as a hedgerow, a row of shrubs or trees enclosing or separating a field. Plants come in all shapes and sizes and can be maintained to a certain shape or height that can help to define areas. Knee-high plants are good directional guides, while waist-high plants are effective for traffic control. Chest-high plants partition patios and sitting areas, and anything eye level and above serves as a complete protective enclosure. Figure 2-4 contains several good suggestions of plants for each height requirement.

Another way to use plants in fence projects is with vines and espaliers (FIG. 2-5). The term *espalier* refers to plants grown in a flat plain that

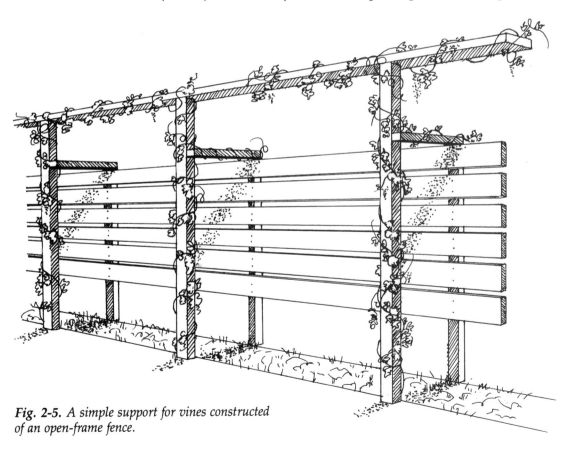

Fig. 2-5. A simple support for vines constructed of an open-frame fence.

Fig. 2-6. A chain-link fence serves the basic function of containment but is usually aesthetically uninteresting.

might attach themselves to a surface for support, such as on a trellis or railing. An ideal fence to enhance with plants is a chain-link fence (FIG. 2-6).

Many people feel that bare, chain-link fences are unattractive, but chain-link has the added advantage of numerous anchor holds for climbing or training plants. Imagine the difference and impact a flowering vine such as clematis can make to this otherwise plain fence.

Choosing a style

Personal preference is one of the strongest forces that dictates the selection of a fence style. While a fence might be required to screen out an objectionable view or provide security, the style will be dictated by individual taste and architectural preferences. Another common variable that affects style is the directional control of strong winds, or wind baffling. Louver-styled fences break the force of strong winds, providing gentle breezes to patio and deck areas. Solid panel fences, such as a picket fence, basketweave, plastic panel, or bevel siding, afford complete protection from strong, harsh winds.

Temperature and wind will affect the configuration of a fence. A solid fence will cause the wind to jump over the fence, creating a trap or pocket of air on the inside. This pocket will be slightly warmer than without the fence for a distance approximately equal to the fence height. To get a more uniform and higher increase in temperature, construct a baffled fence to direct the wind up and over, creating no air pockets. A 45° baffle installed on the top of the fence facing into the wind will yield the greatest protection, increasing the comfort zone equal to more than twice the fence height.

The style of fence does not usually affect the steps required for installation. Fences are usually constructed in panels of varying lengths that are then hung or supported between posts. Two exceptions, discussed later in the chapter, are a split-rail fence and a chain-link fence. These panels can be constructed on site or in advance of installation. After reviewing the examples in FIGS. 2-7 through 2-16, it will become obvious that fences share similar elements.

In many areas, preconstructed and ready-to-install panels are available through fence companies or lumberyards. For those of you who prefer to build from scratch rather than buying a preassembled kit, this next section is for you.

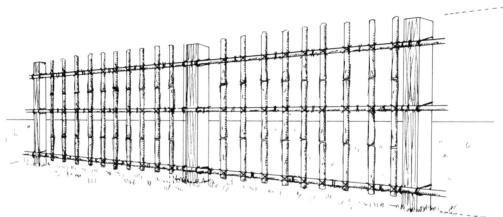

Fig. 2-7. Bamboo poles laced together make an interesting fence.

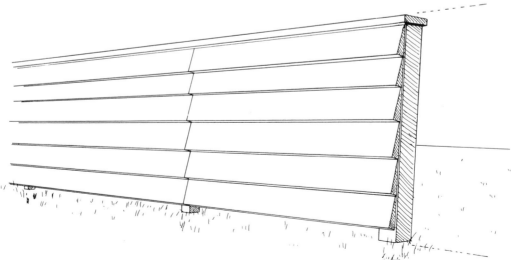

Fig. 2-8. A solid fence is made more interesting by overlapping the horizontal pieces.

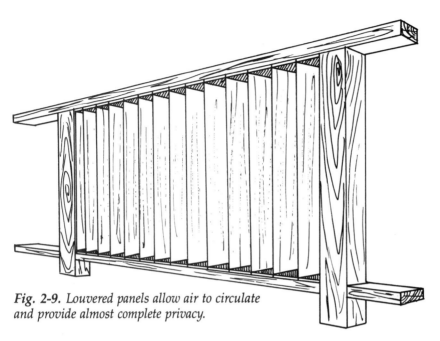

Fig. 2-9. *Louvered panels allow air to circulate and provide almost complete privacy.*

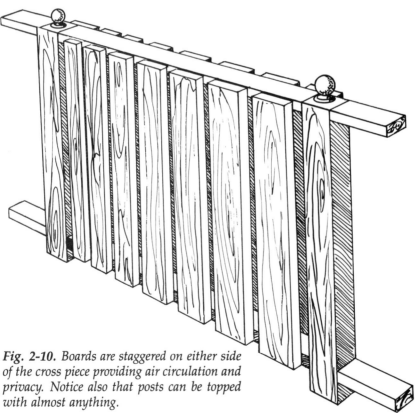

Fig. 2-10. *Boards are staggered on either side of the cross piece providing air circulation and privacy. Notice also that posts can be topped with almost anything.*

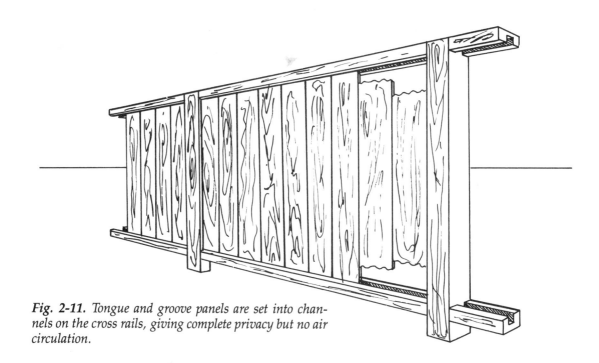

Fig. 2-11. *Tongue and groove panels are set into channels on the cross rails, giving complete privacy but no air circulation.*

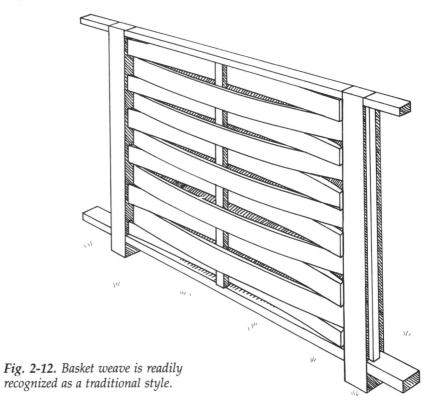

Fig. 2-12. *Basket weave is readily recognized as a traditional style.*

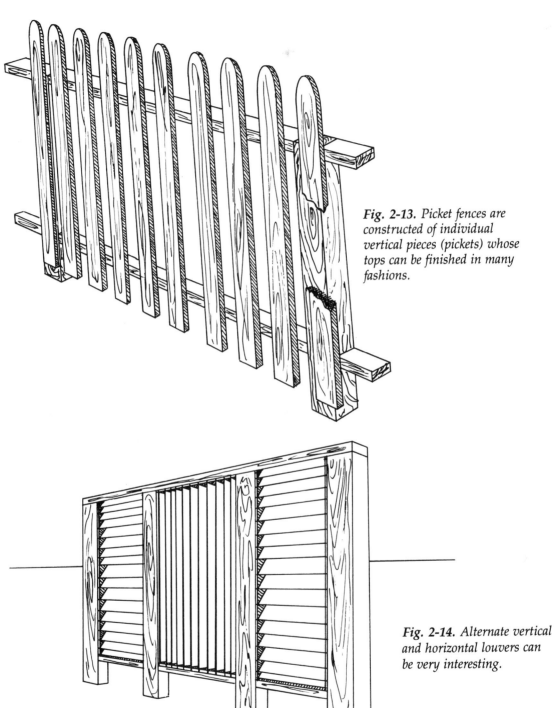

Fig. 2-13. Picket fences are constructed of individual vertical pieces (pickets) whose tops can be finished in many fashions.

Fig. 2-14. Alternate vertical and horizontal louvers can be very interesting.

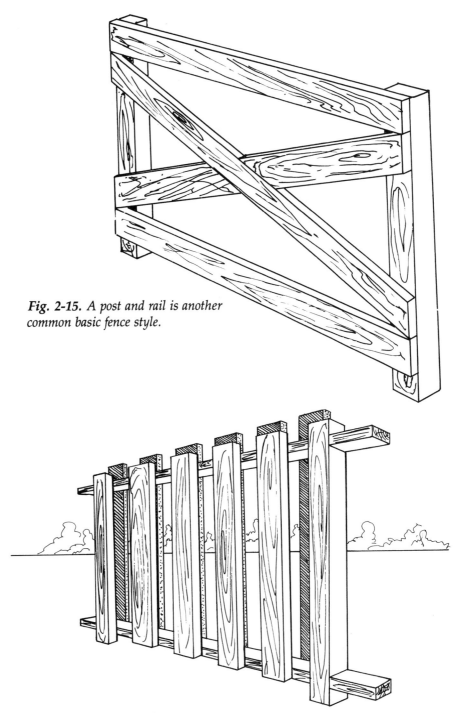

Fig. 2-15. A post and rail is another common basic fence style.

Fig. 2-16. Alternate width boards are faced on either side of the cross rail providing privacy, air circulation, and a unique individual style.

Basic construction

Once you have decided on a fence style, the first thing to do is set the fence posts. In most cases, the posts will be 4×4s of redwood, cedar, or pressure-treated to resist decay. For rustic fences, small-diameter cedar trees might be used for fence posts. Your design will show you the location of the posts in relationship to each other and to property lines or buildings. When transferring these locations to your yard, make certain the fence is on your property and conforms to any restrictions as regulated by local codes.

Drive a stake in the ground at one end of the fence line. Attach a string line and stretch it along the proposed fence line. Secure the string to a stake a few feet longer than the total length of the fence. Following your design's post spacing (usually in increments of 6 or 8 feet), mark the string with pieces of masking tape. Drive a stake in the ground below each mark. Suspending a plumb bob from the string line might be useful in locating the exact position of each post.

After marking the location of all posts, holes must be dug. It is important that all holes be dug to the same depth so that the posts' heights are uniform. Several variables determine the depth of post holes. A tall fence (4 to 6 feet high) requires a hole at least 2 feet deep, while a fence less than 4 feet might only require an 18-inch-deep hole. In areas where frost is a problem, the hole must be deep enough to anchor the post below the frostline. If you are digging more than a few holes and the soil is relatively rock-free, it might be useful to rent a power auger.

Once all the holes are dug, it is time to set the posts. To maintain fence posts at a uniform height, you'll need to establish an additional string line as a guide. Set the first corner post in position, checking that it is plumb and at the required height. Attach a string line 6 inches below the top of the post. Stretch the line to the corner post at the far end of the fence. Measure 6 inches from the top of the post and make a mark. Attach the string line at this mark. With help from an assistant, adjust the height of the post in the ground until the line is level. Secure this post in place using temporary anchor braces or by backfilling the hole. Check carefully to make sure the post is plumb.

Mark all fence posts 6 inches below the top of each post. As you set the posts, align the marks with the string line to ensure that all posts are at the same height. Backfill the bottom of each post hole with 2 to 4 inches of coarse gravel. The amount of stone you'll need will depend on the adjustment needed to align the height mark with the string line.

Once posts are set at the proper height, add an additional 2 inches of coarse gravel in the hole. In areas free of frost heaving or where soil is stable, holes can be backfilled with a soil/gravel mix. Add the coarse soil/gravel mix to each hole in small quantities. As you backfill, tamp the soil firmly with a 2×4. Check posts for plumb, spacing, and alignment along the fence line as you tamp.

In areas troubled by frost heaving, concrete collars are poured around each fence post to ensure that posts hold firmly. After the coarse gravel layer, concrete is added to within 2 to 3 inches of the ground surface. Before the concrete cures completely, adjust the post plumb, in the right location, and in line. After the concrete is completely cured, soil can be added in each hole to ground level. Curing should be allowed to occur for at least two days.

Hanging fence panels

The final step is building or hanging fence panels. Panels are set between posts, and one side is tacked in place at the proper height using an 8d galvanized nail. With the use of a carpenter's level, adjust the height of the free end until the panel is level, and tack in place using an 8d galvanized nail. Predrill three 1/16-inch pilot holes in each end support for every panel. Secure panels to posts using 2 1/2-inch galvanized deck screws. If you are building your panels on site, horizontal top and bottom rails are attached and leveled first. Vertical and/or horizontal face boards (as dictated by the style) are then secured to the top and bottom rails.

Chain-link fences

Chain-link fencing is usually purchased in rolls of 50 feet or more and is attached to posts with metal clips. Corner posts need to be set in concrete to help support the weight of the entire length. On long runs, it is advisable to set all posts in concrete. Otherwise, use the method for securing posts as described in the preceding section.

After all posts are set and secure, the fence is unrolled along the fence line. With the help of an assistant, stand the fence up and attach to the posts starting at a corner or gate post. Stretch the fence and securely attach it to each post before continuing to the next post.

Split-rail fences

Another common fence style is split rail, and its installation is unique. Posts are set in place individually with each section of rail. Starting at one corner, install the first post securely, and insert rails into the post. At the end of the rail length, dig a hole for the next post. Holes need to be large enough to shift the post, insert rails, and then straighten. When this post is in position with rails inserted, backfill it with gravel and soil until secure.

Insert the next section of rails into the second post. Dig a hole at the end of the second section of rails. Install the third post and insert the second section of rails. This procedure continues until all rails and posts are installed.

Constructing gates

Many fence projects require that garden gates be constructed. Gates can be simple and function only to allow passage through the fence or they can be ornate with elaborate focal points. In either case, the basic function of a gate is to get from one side of a fence to the other and, as such, they must work in all types of weather.

A gate that has been built improperly might not close properly or, more frustrating, swell in wet weather and not open. All hardware used in gate construction (as with any garden construction) must be resistant to rust. Brass, cadmium, zinc, or galvanized metals are acceptable. If premade gate panels are not available, the following steps can guide you in constructing your own gate.

Gate posts must be secured in concrete to ensure that they support the gate for many years. Dig post holes 2 feet deep and backfill with concrete as you did with the fence posts. A comfortable width for people passage is $3^1/2$ feet. If you have furniture or garden equipment that must pass through the gate, make sure the opening is large enough to allow easy passage.

Gates larger than 4 feet might be better handled with a two-part gate. Sections need not be of equal width because each section will swing securely and freely from its own post anchor. As with fence posts, gate posts must be plumb and in line. Care should be taken that the distance between gate posts is equal at the top and bottom of the posts.

Build a frame using 2×4s similar to that of your fence (redwood, cedar, or pressure-treated). The frame will be as wide as your gate opening less any space required for your hinge and $1/2$- to $3/4$-inch swing space on the latch side. This space is needed to prevent the gate from nicking or binding on the latch post. When cutting your lumber and assembling, it is important to keep everything square. Secure all frame members using $2^1/2$-inch galvanized deck screws.

Gate sagging is a common problem and can be avoided by cross bracing. This can be accomplished using a 2×4 set diagonally in the gate frame from the bottom hinge corner to the top corner on the latch side. An equally satisfactory method of bracing is to secure a cable and turnbuckle to the gate frame. The action of the cable is to pull up the low corner and must be attached diagonally from the top hinge corner to the lower corner on the latch side.

Fit the frame into the opening, lining it up with the gate posts. Using hinges that you chose earlier, attach the gate to the gate post with anchors large enough to support the weight and constant action of the gate. Check to see that gate frame is level, square, and swings freely.

Attach the panels to the gate frame using galvanized nails or screws. Check that all pieces are either level or plumb, as required, and that they clear the ground or walkway to allow the gate to swing freely.

Install the latch, making sure that the anchor screws, nails, or bolts hold the latch securely. The latch will get a lot of use and can take a beating so be sure it is secure to provide years of trouble-free service.

It is wise to use stock sizes of materials when designing fence panels. Designing a 3-×-6-foot panel using plywood would be wasteful because a sheet of plywood is 4×8 feet. Stock sizes cannot always be used, but they can save material and labor when they are available.

Living fences

Living fences never need to be painted, only occasionally pruned. If selected properly, the amount of care can be minimized. Some typical choices are privet, tallhedge, Russian olive, cherry laurel, hemlock, and yew. Avoid bargain "miracle" fences offered at low prices through some nursery suppliers. The ads praise the rapid growth of these plants. The only problem being that they continue to grow. Any attempt to control or remove these hedges is usually unsuccessful and if it is a rose hedge with thorns, a very disagreeable job.

3

Patios

Unlike a deck, a patio is an expanded living space installed at ground level. Patios are often used for family entertainment and parties. They can provide a secluded environment for conversation and relaxation and are a good place to curl up with a book, recline in a lounge chair, sunbathe, or barbecue.

Patios can provide a sense of direction, leading people to areas that might not otherwise be obvious. A sheltered niche in a garden corner or under a tree might provide a stopping point to gaze, chat, or spend time in solitude.

Finally, patios help to reinforce the character of a particular setting. The type of paving, its pattern, finish, and edgings, all have an enormous effect on the mood or character of a particular surrounding.

Patios can be constructed of flagstone, slate, cobblestone, brick, poured concrete, and concrete pavers, but rarely of wood. When choosing a material, it is a good idea to think simple. Avoid too many textures and colors in one space, and try to use materials that are readily available locally. The cost of any material rises quickly as the distance from the source increases.

Constructing a brick or flagstone patio

While this section focuses on installing brick and flagstone, other appropriate surface materials might include cobblestone, wood rounds, precast concrete slabs, or other locally available materials. The construction procedures will be the same regardless of the materials used (except poured concrete pads, which are discussed in detail later in the chapter).

The first step is to draw a detailed sketch of your proposed project. Use an appropriate scale on graph paper, such as 1 square equals 1 foot. Determine the square footage of your design by multiplying the length times the width. The more accurately you measure and calculate, the easier to accurately order supplies.

Once you have finished sketching your project, assemble all of the tools you will need. This might include: string line, line level, carpenter's level, hand sledge, 10-×-10-inch hand tamp, circular saw with masonry blades, rubber mallet, broom, goggles, shovel, rake, tape measure, wheelbarrow, knee pads, and square.

Once you have your tools together, assemble the patio materials you'll need—brick or flagstone, coarse aggregate stone for a subbase, sand, and railroad ties (mortar or other edging material) for a retainer.

Types of bricks

Bricks are a very diverse group of building material. They are available in a variety of sizes and types specific to certain building applications, some of which are covered in the following section.

Common bricks Common bricks would include ordinary clay that is molded using no additional colors or textures. They are rough in texture, relatively porous, with a slight, lengthwise bow. Hardness is dependent on the brick's location in relationship to the baking fire. Bricks baked close to the fire are hard while those farther away are softer. Soft bricks are usually less weather-resistant and prone to chipping. Hard-burned bricks, those closest to the fire, are often referred to as *clinker* bricks. Common brick is usually the cheapest brick and should only be considered where they will be sheltered from the weather.

Pressed bricks (face bricks) Pressed brick, or face brick, is smoother and finer in texture than common brick, with well-squared corners and greater size consistency. Uniform color and size make this the brick of choice to face walls.

Firebricks Firebrick is a specially made brick that can be used in hearths and fireplaces. Made of fire-resistant clay, these bricks can withstand the hottest of fires.

Paving bricks Paving brick is an ideal choice for walkways, patios, and driveways. This brick is much harder than other bricks, with both faces smooth and all edges rounded. The size allows for a design pattern in even multiples when laid flat.

Roman bricks Typically used in the construction of walls, Roman brick is longer than ordinary bricks. This brick produces a wall with long, low lines.

SCR bricks For easily laid outdoor walls, SCR brick is an excellent choice. Its size is wider and longer than most bricks and allows for the quick construction of a single brick wall. SCR bricks have vertical holes that make them easy to grip when building a wall. If the wall is a low garden wall, a cap course will be needed to cover the holes.

Used bricks You can often find the demolition of an existing brick structure. Used brick can require a great deal of time and effort to sort, clean, and inspect. If bricks can be cleaned easily and are not badly chipped or damaged, you might be able to save considerable money over the cost of new brick. Sometimes, cost and effort are not important because the look and feel used brick imparts to a garden cannot be duplicated with new brick.

Specialty bricks A special need can be addressed by talking to your local supplier. If the project is small, it is unlikely that a forge will manufacture your specific brick. On large jobs, they might be able to accommodate your needs. Some standard specialty bricks available include rounded corners, coping in different shapes and sizes, and hexagonal paving bricks.

Excavating and grading

If the existing grade is flush with the proposed finished patio grade, soil must be excavated to provide space for the subbase of stone and the surfacing material. If the existing grade is lower than the proposed finished patio grade, backfill, plus a retainer, will be needed below the subbase.

A subbase provides a cushion to minimize the heaving effects of freezing (FIG. 3-1). Generally, a 6-inch layer of course aggregate stone is installed in three layers, firmly tamping each 2-inch layer. The base should extend 6 inches beyond the outside perimeter of your patio or to

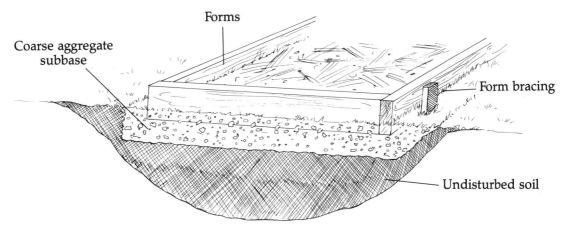

Fig. 3-1. Subbase preparation is important in areas prone to freezing and thawing cycles.

the outer edge of the retainer. One ton of subbase material will cover approximately 100 square feet to a depth of 2 inches. A 3-inch-deep subbase will only cover 75 square feet per ton of material.

Approximately 2 inches of sand is then installed on top of the stabilized subbase. The sand allows brick or flagstone to be placed with grade and pitch adjustments. It also provides adequate runoff away from foundations.

Stabilizing the patio

The perimeter of the patio must be retained, or stabilized, with an edging material. The edge should be approximately 6 inches deep to provide adequate stability. Bricks on end, mortar curbing, or pressure-treated wood are possible materials for adequate edging and retention. Remember, in order for the edging to provide stability, it must be firmly anchored in the ground.

Laying brick or flagstone

Using a string line and line levels as a guideline, lay the surface material slightly higher ($1/4$ inch) than the desired finished level. Tamp the brick, flagstone, or other material into place with a rubber mallet or the handle of a hand sledgehammer. A $1/4$-inch joint space is acceptable and will provide for a neat appearance. Joints will be filled in with clean, dry sand later.

Patterns that minimize the need for cutting simplify installation and optimize installation time (FIG. 3-2). Regardless of the pattern, however, some cuts are unavoidable. Most surfacing materials can be cut using a circular saw with a masonry blade or a hammer and chisel.

A brick set, a wide chisel, is usually used when only a few bricks need to be cut. To cut, place a brick on a firm surface and score along the cutting line with the brick set. Hold the brick set upright with the bevel facing away from you, and then hit firmly with a 5-pound, hand-held sledgehammer. To finish cutting, slightly angle the brick set towards you and hit again.

When a large number of bricks must be cut, a circular saw with an abrasive blade is the tool to use. Construct a jig by nailing two pieces of 2×4 to a piece of plywood spaced apart just enough to allow a brick to rest between them. Set your saw to make a shallow, $1/4$-inch cut and score the brick along the cutting line. Turn the brick over and score the backside. Tap the unwanted piece of brick with a mason's hammer to free the undesired portion.

Because of the variability in surfacing materials, it is always advisable to check with your supplier for recommended methods of cutting.

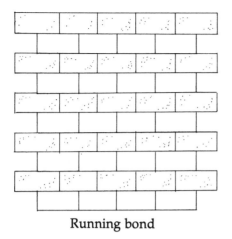

Running bond

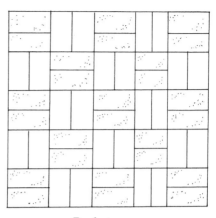

Basket weave

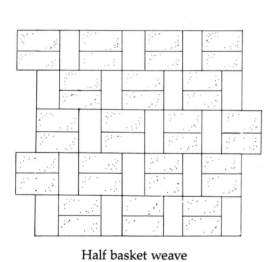

Half basket weave

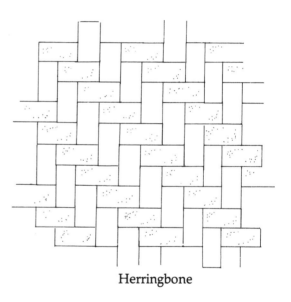

Herringbone

Fig. 3-2. Four common basic brick patterns.

Remember, when cutting any materials, goggles and gloves should be worn to protect eyes and hands.

Finishing up

When all surfacing materials are in place, joints need to be filled with sand to hold materials in place and prevent shifting. Joints are usually 1/4 inch. Lay dry sand on top of the surface and sweep over the surface across all joints. Repeat this process every few weeks for several months until joints are completely filled in (FIG. 3-3).

Constructing a brick or flagstone patio **29**

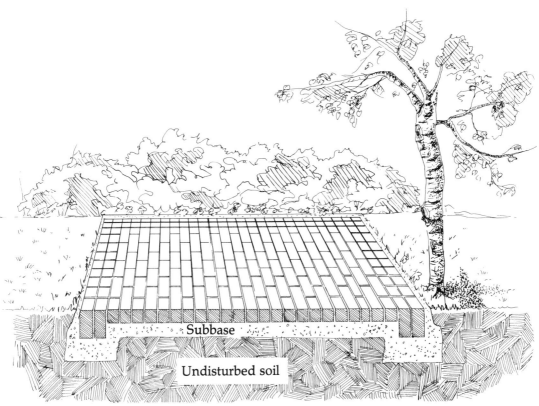

Fig. 3-3. *A completed brick patio using a double row of upright bricks for retention along the edges.*

Constructing a concrete patio

There are four basic ingredients of concrete: cement, aggregate, sand, and water. Portland cement is the "glue" that holds the other parts together. The name *Portland* is derived from the fact that it appears, when cured, like limestone from the island of Portland off the English Coast. It is not a trade name but rather a type of cement that is made by many different manufacturers. However, there are standards for its manufacture, which are set by the U.S. government and the American Society for Testing and Materials (ASTM).

The standard unit is a 94-pound bag equaling 1 cubic foot. Bags must be kept out of damp areas and off the ground and concrete floors during storage. Moisture might be absorbed into the bag causing the cement to become lumpy or solidify completely. Extra care should be taken to see that opened bags are sealed well and that any holes are closed completely. Rather than storing unused portions for any length of time, use the cement to mix a batch of concrete you can use in making your own stepping stones. This process is described later in the chapter.

Two of the ingredients in concrete are actually different sizes of what is typically called aggregates. The fine aggregates are the sands. The best type of sand contains particles of $1/4$ inch and less. These sands are said to have uniform gradation and should be hard enough to withstand freezing and thawing cycles. It is important that this uniform sand mix be kept clean. A poor concrete can result if dirt or other contaminates enter the mix.

The coarse aggregates are usually found as crushed stone or naturally occurring gravel. The same qualities as for sand are needed: uniform gradation, hardness, and cleanliness. The size ranges from $1/4$ inch (the largest sand particle) up to $1/4$ the thickness of the slab.

The final ingredient for concrete is water. Clean, clear water is essential for a good concrete project. The water should be free of alkaline or oils. Never use gasoline or oil containers to measure your water. A well-rinsed milk jug will serve as a good container to supply water to your mix.

Ready-mix concrete

Ready-mix concrete comes to the job site prepared to pour in place and finish. The cost for ready-mix concrete usually fits into the do-it-yourselfer's budget and, because it is ready to use, it works equally well with a homeowner's sometimes overtaxed spare time.

A ready-mix concrete supplier will need to know the amount of concrete needed, the time and place of delivery, and possibly, the maximum coarse aggregate size. Some concrete suppliers will also ask the maximum slump of the mixture as well as the compressive strength your project requires. The compressive strength refers to the load-bearing ability of the concrete. When you explain your project, the supplier should be able to advise you but, as a general rule, a quality concrete project should have a minimum compressive strength of 3,000 psi (pounds per square inch).

The measure of slump, like compressive strength, is something the do-it-yourselfer usually will not calculate. An average maximum slump of 5 inches is suggested for most home projects. Slump is the measure of a concrete mixture's stiffness or wetness. A 1-foot-high cone of concrete is measured for the amount of slump by removing the forming cone. A very wet mixture will slump more than 5 inches, while a dry, stiff mix will slump only 2 to 3 inches. Obviously, if it is too stiff, the concrete will require a great deal of extra effort to spread and finish, while a wet mix will ooze out from around the form.

Concrete is calculated by the cubic yard and the quantity is determined by multiplying the width in feet times the length in feet times the thickness in inches divided by 12. The answer will be the number of cubic feet of material needed. To determine the number of cubic yards you need for your proposed project, divide the number of cubic feet by 27. A patio 10 feet wide, 27 feet long, and 6 inches thick would require 5 cubic yards of concrete (TABLE 3-1).

$$\frac{(10 \times 27 \times 6)}{12} = \frac{135 \text{ cubic feet}}{27} = 5 \text{ cubic yards}$$

Table 3-1. The approximate quantity of excavation or fill needed for various slab sizes and thicknesses.

Slab area	Slab Thickness		
(Square Feet)	2 inch (Cubic Yard)	3 inch (Cubic Yard)	4 inch (Cubic Yard)
10	.06	.09	.12
25	.16	.25	.32
100	.64	.96	1.28
300	1.92	2.88	3.84
500	3.2	4.8	6.4

To estimate the approximate area of a free-form slab, draw the outline on a piece of graph paper and count the number of squares and partial squares covered by the slab. Each partial square is represented as a fractional portion of an entire square. Add the total number of whole squares and fractional squares to find the approximate square footage of the slab.

If the squares on the graph paper represent more than a 1-square-foot area, the total number of squares must be multiplied by that square foot area designation. A free-form slab area with $40^{1}/_{2}$ squares—where each square equals 4 square feet—would equal 162 square feet:

$$40.5 \text{ squares} \times 4 \text{ square feet} = 162 \text{ square feet}$$

Next, multiply the area times the depth of the slab, dividing it by 12 to get the cubic feet of excavation/fill. Again, find the cubic yards by dividing the cubic feet by 27.

$$40.5 \text{ squares} \times 4 \text{ square feet} = 162 \text{ square feet}$$

$$\frac{162 \text{ square feet} \times 4 \text{ inches}}{12} = 54 \text{ cubic feet}$$

$$\frac{54 \text{ cubic feet}}{27} = 2 \text{ cubic yards}$$

When transferring arcs and curves from the graph paper to the yard, you must first determine the radius, the distance from the center of a circle to its outside edge. The center and the radius can be located and marked using a stick and string line. Place the stick at a point equal to the center and with a string, line the length of your radius, scribe a mark on the ground at the end of the string (see FIG. 3-4).

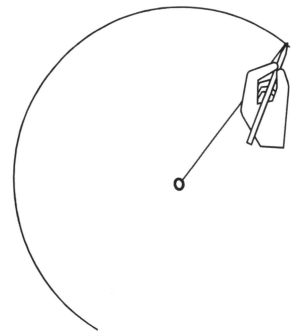

Fig. 3-4. String line stick method of transferring curves and arcs to your working area.

The maximum coarse aggregate size should be equal to $1/4$ of a slab's thickness. In our patio example of a 6-inch-thick slab, the maximum coarse aggregate size would be $1^1/2$ inches.

It is always best to order concrete at least a day before you need it, longer if possible. Make certain that you are ready on the date you select for concrete delivery. Have ready the manpower and any tools you need to rent or borrow. All forms should be in place, braced properly, and areas properly excavated or filled as needed, all of which is discussed later in the chapter.

Pumped concrete

Pumped concrete is ready-mix concrete that is delivered to your project through a flexible hose. The hose can reach through doorways and around corners to place concrete in areas not accessible with a truck. A distance of 250 feet from the pump to the project is not impossible.

Pumping makes placing concrete easier and less time-consuming for these hard-to-reach projects. But time and labor is still needed to finish the work properly. Check with your local supplier or look in the yellow pages for dealers that offer pumping service.

A special mix is used for pumped concrete, so don't forget to tell your supplier your intentions to pump the concrete if your supplier is not doing the pumping.

Air-entrained concrete

Air-entrained concrete contains millions of microscopic air bubbles that act as safety valves for expansion when absorbed water in the concrete freezes. Air-entrained concrete also benefits from greater cohesiveness and freedom from bleeding. Concrete suppliers make this mix using air-entraining portland cement type IA or type IIA or by mixing an air-entraining agent into a mix containing standard portland cement. The agent is usually a vinyl resin.

Check with your local suppliers to see if this or any other air-entraining products are available to the do-it-yourselfer. When mixing this type of concrete, it is essential to have a power mixer, because hand mixing is not vigorous enough.

Pre-packaged concrete

For small quantities of concrete, the best method is to buy pre-packaged mixes. They are sold in 60- or 90-pound bags and are equal to $2/3$ cubic foot of concrete (see TABLE 3-2). These bags are complete except for the water. Gravel or concrete mixes have coarse aggregates and should be used for projects thicker than 2 inches. Projects less than 2 inches thick can use a sand or mortar mix that contains no coarse aggregates. Follow the manufacturer's directions for mixing each bag of product.

Table 3-2. Number of bags needed to yield various cubic feet of concrete depending on the size of bag.

Cubic Feet	60# Bags (yields $1/2$ cu ft/bag)	90# Bags (yields $2/3$ cu ft/bag)
1	2	$1^1/_2$
2	4	3
5	10	$7^1/_2$
10	20	15

Mixing concrete

The most accurate way to mix concrete is to weigh each component in its own container. Using three separate pails, weigh each ingredient, placing a mark on the pail for 1 pound and 5 pounds. A bathroom scale works very well for this purpose. With each pail marked for a 1- and 5-pound quantity, it is simple to mix together any appropriate batch. Table 3-3 lists some suggested proportions based on coarse aggregate size.

Table 3-3. This chart provides components' approximate weights in concrete using the size of the coarse aggregate as a base.

	Component Weights (based on coarse aggregate size)			
Coarse Aggregate (size)	Coarse Aggregate (lb)	Cement (lb)	Sand (wet, lb)	Water (lb)*
3/8"	46	29	53	10
1/2"	55	26	46	10
3/4"	65	25	42	10
1"	70	24	39	9

*Note: 1 gallon of water weighs 8.34 pounds.

Concrete can be mixed using a hoe and a wheelbarrow. Figure 3-5 illustrates the other tools you will need. For larger jobs, a gas or electric-powered mixer can be rented. Place all dry ingredients in the mixer and mix completely. Next, add the water slowly. A dry mix will yield a strong concrete but decrease its workability; a wet mix will increase the workability but reduce strength and durability. A little practice and care will tell you when the mix is just right.

Coloring concrete

Concrete is usually a light gray color. Adding other color to your finished project allows you to integrate concrete with its surroundings for a softer look. The three methods of coloring concrete are:

1. Dyeing, painting, or staining the finished surface.
2. Troweling a coloring agent into the finish of fresh concrete.
3. Adding coloring agents to the concrete mix.

Coloring agents are available from your local supplier and are usually mineral oxides specially prepared for concrete use. They can be natural or synthetic but should be formulated for use with concrete. Frequently available colors include black, white, red, cream, and blue (see TABLE 3-4). Mixing two or more colors allows you to be creative with the color hue. Be creative but don't overdo it. Nature's colors and hues are always closely related and usually subtle. To obtain an intense color

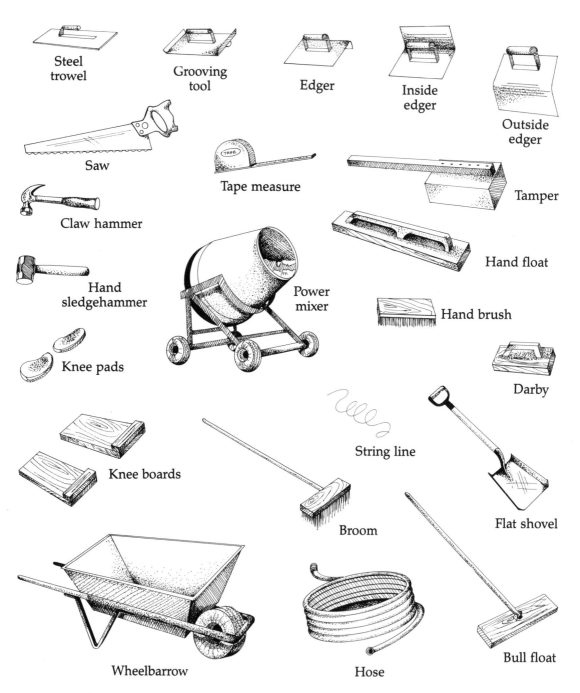

Steel trowel

Grooving tool

Edger

Inside edger

Outside edger

Saw

Tape measure

Tamper

Claw hammer

Hand float

Hand sledgehammer

Power mixer

Hand brush

Knee pads

Darby

Knee boards

String line

Flat shovel

Broom

Wheelbarrow

Hose

Bull float

Fig. 3-5. Tools commonly used in concrete work.

Table 3-4. Typical sources for concrete colors.

Color	Coloring Agent Guide *Material to Provide Color*
Light gray	Normal portland cement
Black	Black iron oxide, carbon black
White	White portland cement, white silica sand
Red	Red oxide of iron
Cream	Yellow oxide of iron
Blue	Cobalt oxide, ultramarine blue

for accent, 10 percent of the weight of the cement can be added. Any more coloring will weaken the finished product.

Blended color Color added to concrete mix must be blended thoroughly. Inadequate mixing can result in patchy, uneven, or streaky color in your paving. If the area to be colored is large, the paving can be poured in two layers. A base layer prepared and installed to within an inch of the top of your forms is set down first. Leveling but no troweling should be done to this layer. The layer should be allowed to set until surface water has evaporated.

The top layer of color should be a standard concrete mix minus the coarse aggregates with a color agent blended in thoroughly. This layer of concrete is placed on top of the first layer and finished by screeding, floating, and troweling.

Troweled color Concrete should be leveled with a bull or hand float and allowed to set until surface water has evaporated. At this stage, the powdered dry coloring agents are shaken evenly over the surface. To facilitate even spreading, the coloring agent is mixed with fine mortar sand in the ratio of 2 parts sand to 1 part color. After the coloring agent has absorbed some moisture from the surface, it should be hand floated into the surface. Repeat the preceding steps using half the quantity of the coloring agent as the first time. Following hand floating, trowel the entire surface. Fifty pounds of the sand/coloring agent mix will color approximately 100 square feet of surface.

Painted color Painted color is usually employed on previously finished concrete. If the surface has been previously painted, careful preparation of the surface is needed. An unpainted surface will still need some preliminary preparation, however. A good source for recommendations on preparing and finishing concrete is your local paint store. They can best advise what products are locally available and effective. Special paints made for concrete should be used and can be applied by brush, roller, or spraying. To achieve maximum longevity, a paint formulated with an epoxy is recommended.

Construction basics

Concrete needs uniform support. Never place concrete on mud, snow, ice, or soft spots. In areas where subsurface water might present a problem, drainage tiles can help drain excess water. The tiles, or any drain bed, must be provided with an adequate reservoir to collect the water runoff.

Any recent excavation should be well compacted to ensure proper support. Trenches for gas, water, or electric lines are all examples of recent excavations that should have the backfill soaked well and tamped (FIG. 3-6). Repeat this process several times and, if possible, over an extended period of several months. If you do not have time to extend the compaction period, be certain to use reinforcing rebar or wire (discussed further in the chapter) in the slab above these points. Any future settling creates the potential for cracks and sinking in unreinforced slabs.

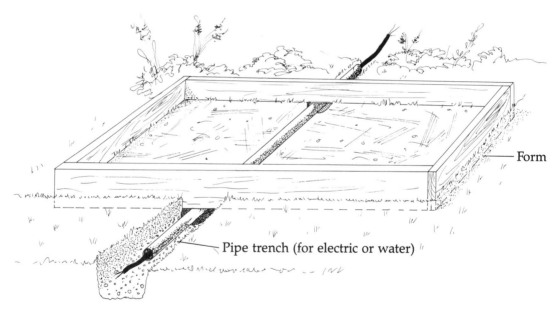

Fig. 3-6. *Pipes for water or wiring should be installed before pouring the concrete. Encasing wires in a pipe makes repairs and additions easier.*

Forming

Forms need not always be thought of as "throwaway lumber." Redwood, cedar, cyprus, or pressure-treated lumber form boards can be incorporated into the design of your project (see FIG. 3-7). If forms are to remain as part of the design, the exposed surface should be covered to prevent concrete from adhering to, or staining, the boards. Wax paper works well for this purpose. It can be removed easily after the concrete has been ini-

Fig. 3-7. *If boards are to be left in your project as part of the design, the addition of ''handles'' placed on the inside are useful in securing boards. Handles can be easily provided by driving nails on the inside of the cross boards.*

tially finished. If any concrete gets on the form during pouring and placing, remove it as soon as possible.

If your design was planned in units, setting up the forms will be easier. The units will allow you to fill and completely finish portions of the entire project. This way, large areas can be finished in phases over several days or weeks.

If the patio will butt against the house, mark the foundation wall, the wall's plaster lip, or any other predominant feature that is installed level, with a pencil 2 inches down from the doorway. Center the doorway, or other adjoining structure, then snap a chalk line between these two marks to center the slab. These marks will also establish the high point when grading the site so that the slab pitches away from the foundation.

Forms should be braced with wooden stakes on the outside and level with the top of the form board (see FIG. 3-8). Steel stakes are very expensive and should only be used in especially rocky, hard terrain where wood stakes would splinter or break. Place stakes every 3 feet or so along forms to guarantee that none bow, are knocked out of position, or snap. Never place stakes any more than 4 feet apart. Stakes should be secured to the form boards using double-headed nails so that they can be removed easily after concrete has set. Nail one end of the form board to the first stake at the desired level. Using a carpenter's level or mason's line as a guide, nail the far end of the form board securely to a stake.

Place stakes close together on curves. Wet concrete exerts a great deal of pressure on forms and curves are particularly vulnerable. If not properly anchored, concrete can push forms out of alignment. Thin plywood overlapped in two to three layers will allow you to form any curves in

Fig. 3-8. All forms must be supported securely with stakes until concrete cures completely.

your project. Soak wood thoroughly in water before bending it in place and securing it with stakes. It is much more pliable this way and won't crack or split as easily.

Expansion joints, predetermined cracking zones, should be considered for almost all concrete projects because concrete expands during hot weather and contracts during cold weather. If a slab is confined on all four sides, cracking is inevitable. Patio slabs, however, are usually open on two or three sides and can generally expand and contract without cracking.

If your patio will butt against another slab, however, such as an adjoining walkway, an expansion joint must be installed between the slabs. A clear piece of 2-×-4 redwood, cedar, or pressure-treated wood will serve as an adequate expansion joint. Expansion joint felt and redwood benderboard are two additional choices.

If drainage is a concern for your patio, plastic drainpipe can be placed inside forms to direct water runoff from beneath the slab. When concrete is poured and placed, be sure that drainpipe is completely covered. If it is positioned too high in the slab, a weak spot will develop that could lead to cracks. Once forms are placed, it is time to prepare and grade the base.

Grading

Existing landscape, such as a flower bed, doorway, or an adjoining walkway, might sit too high (or low) in relation to where you want the top surface of the patio to be located. In this case, you will have to grade and level the planned patio area to mesh with its surroundings. Also, if the patio will be next to the house, it must pitch away so that water can run off from around the foundation toward the yard, a drain, or the street (see TABLE 3-5).

Table 3-5. Typical recommendations for slabs based on their application.

	Slab Recommendations		
Slab Use	Minimum Thickness	Minimum Width	Slope
Driveways	4″ (cars)	8′-9′ (1 car)	1/4″ per foot
	5″ (trucks)	15′-18′ (2 cars)	14% of max. grade
Sidewalks	3″ (foot traffic)	2′-3′	1/4″ per foot
Patios	4″	according to use	1/4″ per foot

Remember to allow for proper pitch away from buildings. While patios generally only pitch away from the house to provide drainage, driveways and most walkways should have a crown in the center. This crown provides drainage for both sides of a slab. The slab should be at least 2 inches below the floor level to prevent water, dust, and debris from coming in through the doorway. Patios should pitch away from the house or other permanent structure at a rate of 1 inch every 10 feet.

Preparing the base

Once all forms are secured and the site is graded, you still have one more chore to do before you can begin pouring the concrete. Concrete needs water in the mix to help it cure properly. If the soil you will be placing concrete on is very dry, the soil will act like a wick and draw water out of the concrete. When this happens, the concrete cannot cure properly and your finished project is weakened. To avoid this, soak the area inside the forms with water the day before placing concrete. Apply enough water to evenly saturate the site several inches, not create a mud puddle.

Heat can also cause a problem for proper finishing and curing. On days you expect very hot weather, try to pour concrete in early morning. The earlier concrete is placed in forms, the easier it will be to finish. Temporary shade might provide relief for hot days if concrete can't be placed early in the day.

Freezing conditions can also cause problems. If the concrete freezes before it cures, the final slab, when it does cure, will be weakened. Postpone the job if freezing conditions will occur before curing, about 5 to 7 days.

Placing concrete

Before you begin to actually place concrete, you should have on sturdy rubber work boots and heavy rubber gloves to protect your skin from any damage. You should also have someone there to help you throughout the pour and initial finishing stages. Wet concrete is very heavy and you will need help maneuvering the concrete and screed board.

Check the consistency of concrete before you begin placing it into forms. If the concrete flows too easily, it probably contains too much water. Force concrete into all of the corners. Always place the concrete full depth against a form and work backwards into your slab area.

Finishing

The first chore to finishing concrete is smoothing concrete with a screed. With an assistant, seesaw a long, straight 2×4, or screed, across the top of form boards. Push any excess concrete ahead of the screed and fill any low areas behind the screed. Screed the surface a second time, making sure that it is level to the top of the forms across the entire area.

For large slabs, a bull float is used to do the initial floating after screeding. A bull float is a long-handled float, usually with a 4-foot-long wooden or aluminum blade, used to smooth out irregularities in a slab's surface. On sidewalks and surfaces that can be reached easily, a darby, worked in overlapping arcs, works just as well. Float the slab with a wood or magnesium float after surface water has evaporated (FIG. 3-9).

After the initial floating is complete, forms can be removed from all sections that have throwaway forms. Remove the coverings of permanent form boards and clean any boards that might have concrete on them.

When the surface water has evaporated and the slab can hold your weight with only 1/4-inch boot depression, final finishing can start. Remove your boot print immediately, however.

Final finishing

Final finishing involves floating and edging. Edges are placed on the slab using a special edging tool. Working this tool back and forth along edges results in smooth, rounded edges that will not easily chip. Control joints, or expansion joints, can be cut into the slab at this time using a tool that will cut the joint 1/4 the slab's thickness.

The final floating of the slab is usually followed by a brooming. Too smooth a surface can become dangerously slick outdoors. Brooming also hides imperfections such as trowel and float lines. A stiff-bristled broom swept lightly across the surface leaves a fine texture. The harder you broom, the more coarse the texture produced. Avoid overworking the concrete, however, because this will bring too much of the cement paste, or cream, to the surface. Overworking a slab leads to dusting, crazing (hairline cracking), and scaling.

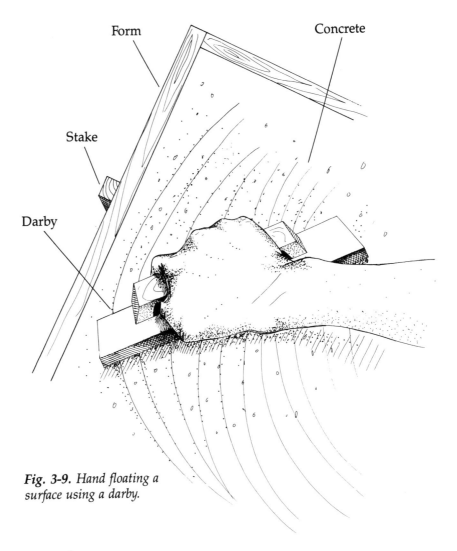

Form

Concrete

Stake

Darby

Fig. 3-9. Hand floating a surface using a darby.

Exposed aggregate

A common finish for slabs is exposed aggregate. This finish can be obtained by mixing the concrete using a coarse, round aggregate and removing, at the final floating, the cement that covers the top layer of aggregate.

An alternate method involves "seeding" the slab with aggregates. Spread, or seed, your aggregate of choice evenly on top of recently screeded concrete. Using a flat board, work the aggregates into the surface of the concrete, making sure that they are firmly embedded and even with the top of slab forms.

Allow the concrete to set up until it is able to support your weight on a board. At this point, float the surface with a metal float so that the aggregates are buried just below the surface and are completely surrounded by concrete. After about an hour, you'll be able to start exposing the aggregate. This is done with a stiff-bristled broom and water spray from a garden hose to brush and wash away the top layer of cream to expose the aggregates.

Concrete reinforcing

Most do-it-yourself concrete jobs benefit more from extra thickness than from steel reinforcement. The cost of extra thickness is oftentimes less than that of steel reinforcing.

Three specific project types will, however, need steel reinforcing. The first type does not involve the do-it-yourselfer, because it deals with the engineered reinforcement of buildings and load-bearing structures such as columns and beams. The other two types, described in detail in the following section, are light reinforcement and heavy reinforcement.

Light reinforcement   Light reinforcement is obtained with a welded wire fabric. This material looks like a screen, but with heavier wire and larger spaces between the wires. Welded wire is used to reinforce some walls and slabs. It cannot prevent cracking, but the slab will not fall apart because the wire holds it together.

Steel mesh is sold in rolls or sheets depending on the gauge (thickness) of the wire. Gauges of 6, 8, and 10 are common with #6 wire being thicker than #10 wire. The other measurement used for welded-wire fabric is the size of the gap. A spacing of 6×6 inches is the most common.

Place the roll inside your forms and cut it to size with wire cutters. The fabric should be held off the ground approximately 1/2 the thickness of the slab so that when the slab cures, the reinforcing wire is in the middle of the concrete (FIG. 3-10 shows the proper placement of reinforcing screen).

Heavy reinforcement   If a slab is to receive heavy vehicular traffic or a small wall is needed to hold back a low grade, reinforcing is best obtained through steel bar called *rebar*. Rebar is commonly available smooth or deformed (with lugged ridges). Smooth bars are usually 3/8 inch or smaller. Deformed bars are sold in 20-foot lengths of various multiples of 1/8-inch thicknesses. Each size is assigned a number that indicates the number of eighths in the bar. A #3 bar is 3/8 inch thick and a #4 bar is 4/8 inch thick or 1/2 inch thick. Some concrete suppliers will cut specific lengths or bend lengths of rebar to your needs. This service might involve a charge, however, so check before you get surprised. Once cut or bent, you own it—they don't want it back.

Rebar should be laid inside forms, crisscrossing in a grid pattern.

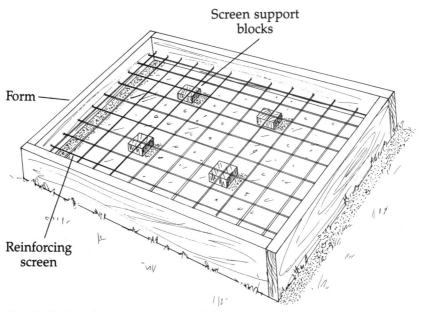

Screen support
blocks

Form

Reinforcing
screen

Fig. 3-10. *Reinforcing screen placed inside the forms and supported off the ground to a depth equal to half the thickness of the slab.*

The grid should be no less than 3 inches square and no more than 3 times the thickness of the slab. A 3-inch-thick slab would have a maximum spacing of 9 inches. Rebars are tied together with wire at all intersections to prevent them from shifting while placing the concrete. Rebar should be positioned about 1/3 of the way down in a slab. Bars would be located, for instance, $1^1/_4$ inches below the surface of a $3^1/_2$-inch slab. Blocks of wood or brick can be used to hold rebar at the desired depth. Pre-built supports might also be available for purchase.

Iron and steel scraps found in your garage or basement can be used for reinforcement instead of rebar, but they should be free of rust, grease, and oil. Dirty metal can cause concrete to weaken and defeat the purpose of reinforcement.

Finishing up

Once final finishing is completed, there is still work to be done. Tools must be thoroughly cleaned of all concrete before it dries and hardens, possibly ruining tools. The slab must be protected for several weeks while it cures. If a slab cures too quickly, as under very hot conditions, it can weaken the slab and cause damage. If the slab should freeze while curing, it will expand and crack also. Therefore, cover the slab with a heavy, rain-proof tarp or canvas that will allow the slab to receive air to cure but not subject it to adverse weather.

Concrete repairs

All concrete projects are susceptible to damage from freezing or other harsh weather conditions and it is not uncommon for chips or cracks to appear, but they should be repaired as soon as the weather will permit. At one time, repairs were a troublesome task. Today, improved vinyl, epoxy, or latex compounds make for stronger and more trouble-free slabs than yesteryear's fix of portland cement and sand.

Vinyl compounds Vinyl patching compounds come ready to use—just add water—and are ideal for rough or pockmarked surfaces. Vinyl can be applied in layers as thin as 1/8 inch. Vinyl is an excellent choice in cold climates because it is not adversely affected by freezing and thawing.

Latex compounds Latex patching compounds are sold complete with a dry mix and a liquid latex. The two are mixed together according to label directions, although these sometimes must be altered because of the job application. A broken corner that needs to be built out will require a stiffer consistency, while small cracks and chips might need a thinner, more flowable mixture. Latex has the ability to be "feathered out" on the edges, meeting surrounding edges smoothly.

Epoxy compounds Epoxy compounds have superior bonding strength and can be used for setting brick, tile, and flagstone; bonding glass, steel, and ceramic tile; and patching concrete. Because it can be "feathered out," concrete does not need to be chipped away from the damaged area. Preparation includes brushing away all loose concrete and dirt and removing any oil or grease from the surface.

It is important to mix compounds in small quantities because they set up very quickly. If the patch cannot be worked quickly, divide the area and use two or more patches. Large repair jobs that require sections of concrete to be replaced are best accomplished using conventional concrete and sand mixes. Patching compounds usually are too expensive and quick-acting for large jobs.

Clean the area to be patched and mix the repair concrete as suggested on the concrete/sand package. In order that the patch holds, the original work must be coated with a bonding agent. Mix portland cement and water into a thick, creamy slurry. Brush the slurry on all surfaces in contact with the patch. Set the patch in place while the slurry is still wet. The slurry needs tooth for grip so, if the surface is smooth, it will need to be acid etched. Consult local concrete suppliers on how to safely acid etch concrete.

Casting paving block

You can avoid the annoyance of what to do with extra concrete from larger projects by being prepared with forms to cast your own stepping stones or paving rocks. The cast blocks can be any size, shape, or color to fit your particular needs. The final shape you choose will depend on your ability to construct an appropriate form. Hexagonal, triangular, octagonal, and diamond shapes are all easily worked. It is also possible to make free-form blocks using pliable form materials.

Tools needed to make your blocks will be the same as for any concrete project. The materials include concrete, either left over from a larger project or prepared in small quantities for this specific purpose, and forms. The forms should be constructed using straight, smooth wood so that the blocks are uniform and easily removed from the forms.

Cut boards to desired lengths to form a box to fit your project. Hinge three corners with the fourth corner fitted with a hasp and securing peg. Once a block has set up sufficiently, it can be removed from the form by pulling the peg, opening the hasp, and unfolding the hinged sides.

A stiff concrete mix allows you to remove and reuse the forms more quickly. To help the forms release cleanly and easily, use wax paper to line the boards. Once the boards are removed, the paper can be stripped away, any remaining paper will disintegrate when the block is set in place.

If you are working on a concrete floor, place a piece of tar paper or plywood on a level surface underneath the form to protect the surface. If you are working on the ground, it will help to prevent too rapid a moisture loss.

Fill forms with your concrete mix, making sure it is packed into all corners. Work the concrete in place and release any trapped air. If reinforcement is to be added, it should be placed so that it is in the middle of the slab. Screed with a zigzag motion across the top of a slightly over-full form with a 2×4. Finish the surface with a float and trowel then broom to give the surface texture.

Just as with a patio slab, blocks can be finished in any one of several colors or as exposed aggregate. The size of a block is dictated by its purpose. All blocks should be cast $2^{1}/_{2}$ to $3^{1}/_{2}$ inches thick. If the blocks are to be stepping stones, they should be uniform and not exceed 16×32 inches. Larger blocks are very heavy and extremely difficult for most do-it-yourselfers to place properly. If the blocks are to be used in a pattern for a walkway or patio, the unit size must be worked out carefully so that the pieces all fit together uniformly. A rule of thumb for rectangular blocks suggests that the length should be no more than two times the width.

Precast paving blocks are commercially available in many areas. Some of these blocks have patterns that the do-it-yourselfer cannot produce. Also, the cost might be comparable to the cost of doing your own, but without all the extra effort.

4

Decks

Decks have been around for many years. Design concepts have traditionally been influenced by Egypt, Greece, China, and Spain. As is true of patios, decks aesthetically enhance a yard as well as providing space to entertain family and friends. These outdoor spaces can be used seasonally for sleeping or stargazing when furnished with cots, hammocks, water beds, or sleeping bags. They can also serve as areas for container gardening of herbs and vegetables. Decks can also ease yard maintenance by acting as lawn substitutes.

When designing a deck, start with your own personal "wish list." The aforementioned are just a few of the many uses of a deck. Other wish-list items might include a barbecue area, reading niche, entry deck, playroom for the children, greenhouse, hot tub, or dog run.

The size and design of your deck is restricted only by your imagination and building ability. When thinking about a deck, it is also important to consider a "roof." A roof could be an umbrella or canvas structure or a natural roof provided by the canopy of a large tree or through lattice and vines.

Parts of a deck

Figure 4-1 depicts the parts of the decks described in detail in the following section:

Ledgers Ledgers are like beams in that they support joists. A deck, however, usually has only one ledger, which attaches the deck to the house.

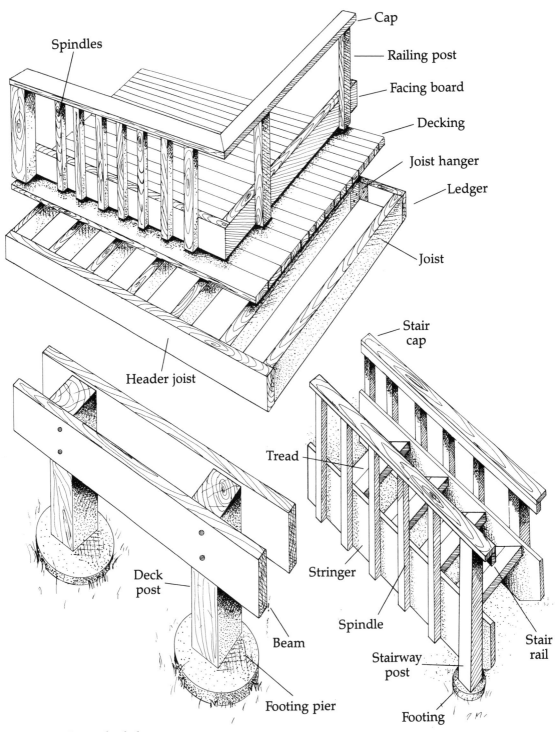

Spindles

Cap

Railing post

Facing board

Decking

Joist hanger

Ledger

Joist

Header joist

Stair cap

Tread

Stringer

Deck post

Beam

Spindle

Stairway post

Stair rail

Footing

Footing pier

Fig. 4-1. Parts of a deck.

Footings Footings, which are always made of concrete, support the weight of the deck while holding the deck posts in place. Post anchors are set into wet concrete so that when concrete cures (hardens), the anchor becomes a permanent part of the footing block. To avoid rusting, these anchors should be made of galvanized steel. A footing generally needs to be deeper in colder climates than in warmer climates. Check your local building codes to determine the depth of footings.

Posts Posts are the structural members of the deck that transfer the weight of the deck to the footings. Beams are attached to the posts using galvanized lag screws. The posts are then nailed to the post anchors using galvanized nails.

Beams Beams are usually constructed of a pair of 2×8s or 2×10s and are attached to the posts using galvanized lag screws. Beams serve as the main structural support for the deck.

Joists Joists are fastened at one end to the ledger and at the opposite end to the header joist. For appearance, the outside joist can be faced (covered) with redwood or cedar. The joists rest on the beams and support the deck boards.

Decking Decking refers to the top surface of the deck. Each pattern gives the deck its own unique and individual character. Deck boards can be run in many patterns across the joists, but if the boards are shifted from a straight pattern, additional joist supports might be needed. Deck boards are attached to the joists using galvanized screws or nails.

Railings Railings might be required by local code for any deck constructed above ground level. The need for railings and the requirements of construction can be determined by a call or visit to your local building code office. The standard parts of a railing include railing posts and spindles, which are attached to the header and outside joists, a horizontal rail, and a cap.

Steps Steps are easily constructed using a pair of stringers attached to the side of a deck and treads attached to the stringers with metal cleats. Stringers can also be cut out for the treads, giving a more finished appearance. This process is covered later in the chapter.

Allowable spans for decking, joists, beams, and the size of posts depend on the size, grade, and spacing as well as the wood type. Some woods, such as southern pine, will allow greater spans than less dense woods such as cedar or redwood. Regardless of the wood type, lumber should be No. 2 grade or better.

Post size

Post size is determined by first calculating the load area of your deck. To find the load area, multiply the distance between posts by the distance between beams. The load area for a deck with posts spaced 6 feet apart and beams 10 feet apart is 60. If your deck is to be less than 6 feet above grade, the recommended post size would be a 4×4. See FIG. 4-2 for other load-area, post-size specifications. Always use the next highest load area to determine post size. A general rule of thumb indicates that the minimum dimension of a post should be the same as the beam width.

Wood Type	Post Size	Load area beam spacing x post spacing (sq.ft.)									
		36	48	60	72	84	96	108	120	132	144
Southern Pine	4"x4"	Height to 12'				Height to 10'			Height to 8'		
	4"x6"					Height to 12'				Height to 10'	
	6"x6"								Height to 12'		
Cedar or Redwood	4"x4"	to 12'	to 10'		Height to 8'			Height to 6'			
	4"x6"			to 12'		Height to 10'			Height to 8'		
	6"x6"						Height to 12'				

Fig. 4-2. Recommended post size based on load.

Beam spans or post spacing

The maximum allowable span of beams depends on the size and spacing of the beams. For instance, 4-×-6 beams with a space between beams of 12 feet (joist span), would require a post spacing of no more than 5 feet along each beam. Conversely, posts that are 10 feet apart with 4-×-10 beams would have a maximum joist span of 10 feet (see FIG. 4-3).

A span is the distance along a deck member from one support to the next. A joist span would then be the length of the joist as measured from one beam to the next beam.

Maximum joist span

Joist span is based on the variables of joist size and spacing between joists. A deck with a 2-×-8 joist spaced 24 inches on center requires supports (beams) no more than 10 feet 6 inches apart (the span of the joist). Most joists are set either 16 or 24 inches on center with additional bracing when unique deck patterns are used (see FIG. 4-4). When you want to cantilever a deck, the joist can extend beyond the last beam a distance

Wood Type	Beam Size	Spacing between posts (ft)								
		4	5	6	7	8	9	10	11	12
Southern Pine	3"x8"	8' span								
	3"x10"	11'	10'	9'	8' span		7' span		6' span	
	3"x12"		12'	11'	10'	9' span		8' span		
Cedar or Redwood	3"x8"	7'	6'							
	3"x10"	9'	8'	7'	6' span					
	3"x12"	11'	10'	9'	8'	7' span			6' span	

Fig. 4-3. Recommended post spacing along a beam.

Wood Type	Joist size	Joist Span (based on size of joist & spacing between joists)		
		16	24	32
Southern Pine	2"x6"	9'9"	7'-11"	6'-2"
	2"x8"	12'10"	10'-6"	8'1"
	2"x10"	16'15"	13'4"	10'4"
Cedar or Redwood	2"x6"	7'9"	6'2"	5'0"
	2"x8"	10'2"	8'1"	6'8"
	2"x10"	13'0"	10'4"	8'6"

Fig. 4-4. Joist span guidelines.

equal to 1/3 the total length of the joist. A 6-foot overhang is all that could be cantilevered when an 18-foot joist is used.

Stair recommendations

When building stairs, remember that a 2-×-10 stringer can be used for spans (runs) up to 6 feet and a 2×12 should be used when the span (run) exceeds 6 feet.

General construction guidelines

The following are some general guidelines for deck construction:

- Use nonstaining fasteners, such as aluminum, copper, or galvanized steel.
- It is always better to fasten a thinner board to a thicker board.
- To reduce the splitting of boards when nailing: a) blunt the nail point; b) predrill nail holes; c) use thinner diameter nails; d) use greater space between nails
- On 4- and 6-inch-wide boards, a minimum of two nails should be used. Three nails are recommended as a minimum for 8- and 10-inch-wide boards.
- When using lag screws, flat washers should be placed under the head. Predrilled holes for lag screws make insertion easier and fastening stronger.
- When using bolts, flat washers should be placed under the head and nut of machine bolts, but need only be underneath nuts on a carriage bolt.
- Never use wood in direct contact with soil unless wood is suitably preserved, such as by pressure treating.

When deciding on the final size of a deck, these minimum recommendations should be considered:

- A person sitting at a table requires 2 feet 2 inches front to back and 2 feet 3 inches side to side.
- The most comfortable seat height is 18 inches. Typical table height is 29 to 30 inches. A person sitting in a deck chair requires 40 inches front to back.
- A standard, round picnic table has a 42-inch diameter. A chair pulled up to a standard picnic table takes up 20 inches front to back so that a picnic table with a chair on each side has a diameter of 82 inches.
- A chaise lounge is usually 6 feet long and $2^1/2$ feet wide.

After you've decided on a design for your deck (see FIGS. 4-5 and 4-6), you need to follow an organized sequence for the construction. The following section contains sequential steps to complete a deck, all of which are covered in detail.

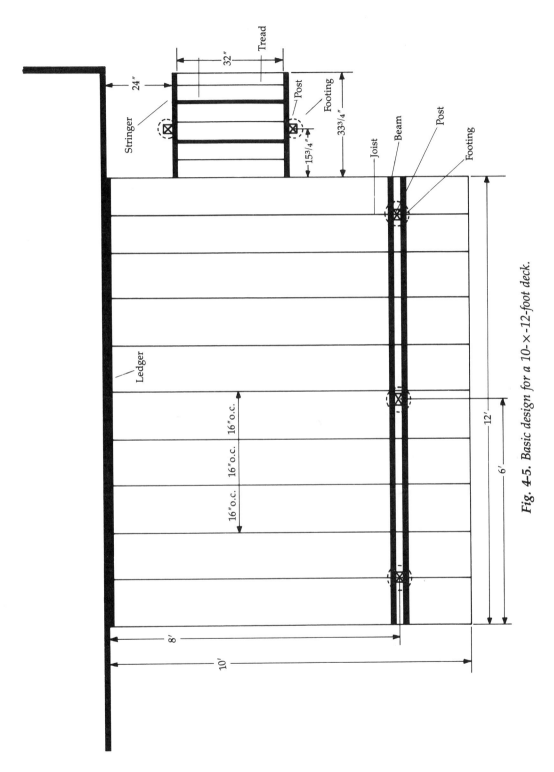

Fig. 4-5. *Basic design for a 10-×-12-foot deck.*

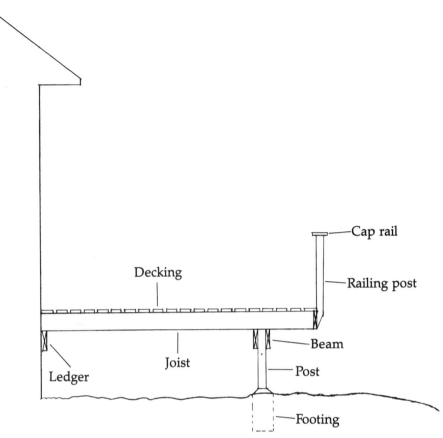

Fig. 4-6. *Side view of deck members.*

Attaching a ledger to siding

In order to lay out a deck properly, the ledger must first be attached to the house. Because the ledger secures the deck to the house and supports one end of all joists, it must be attached securely to the framing members of the house. To prevent melted snow or rain from seeping into the house, the deck surface should be 1 inch below the indoor floor level. To do this, the top of the ledger must be set so that it not only allows for the 1-inch drop, but for the thickness of the deck boards (FIG. 4-7).

Locate the position of the ledger on the house (FIG. 4-8). Draw an outline using a chalk line to snap the horizontal guidelines. The cutout area should be large enough to accommodate the overall width of the deck, including any decorative facing boards.

Cut along guidelines with a circular saw (FIG. 4-9). The blade depth should be set so that it cuts only as deep as the thickness of the siding.

Fig. 4-7. Ledger in position and level.

Corners that are inaccessible to the circular saw can be removed using a hammer and chisel. Removing the siding allows the ledger to be attached flat to the house.

The ledger of pressure-treated lumber is cut to length. Keep in mind that, because the outside joists are attached to the ends of the ledger, it must be shorter than the overall deck width by the thickness of 2 joists (FIG. 4-10). If the overall width of the deck is 10 feet, the ledger would be only 9 feet 9 inches long, because two 2×8 joists are 3 inches thick.

Cut a length of flashing with metal snips to install in the top of the opening. Slide the strip up under the siding to help prevent moisture damage to the wood.

Place the ledger under the flashing, flush against the house and in the center of the cutout (FIG. 4-11). Center it so that the joist on each end can be attached. Hold the ledger in place using 12d nails placed randomly across its length.

Drill 1/4-inch pilot holes through the ledger and into the house's header joist (FIG. 4-12). The holes should be in pairs every 2 feet along the length of the ledger. Each pilot hole should be countersunk about a 1/2 inch deep using a 1-inch spade bit. Using a ratchet, install 3/8-×-4-inch galvanized lag screws and washers in each pilot hole.

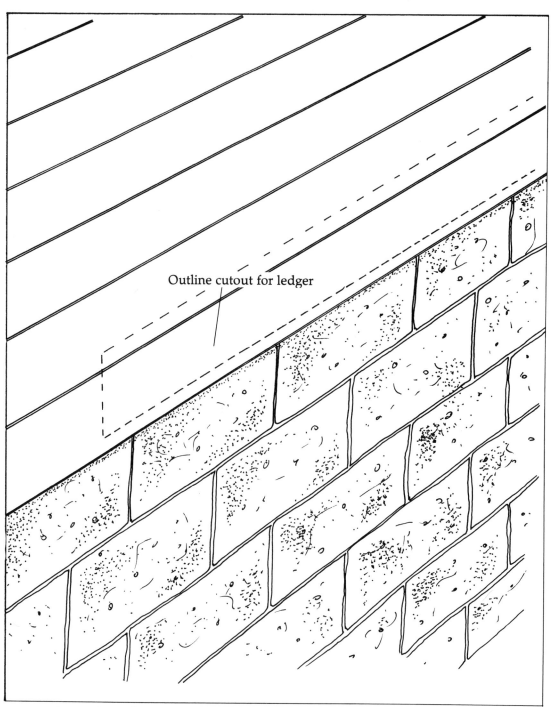

Outline cutout for ledger

Fig. 4-8. Measuring and marking the location of the ledger.

Fig. 4-9. Cut and remove outlined area.

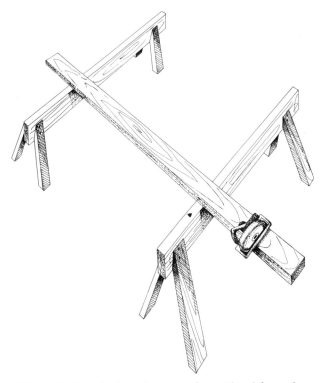

Fig. 4-10. *A pair of sawhorses make cutting jobs easier and safer.*

While all parts are easily accessible, silicon caulk should be used to seal the lag screw heads and a bead applied between the siding and the flashing (FIGS. 4-13 and 4-14).

Attaching a ledger to masonry

A slightly different procedure is used when attaching a ledger to masonry instead of siding. First, anchor holes must be drilled in the ledger before it is placed in position. With the ledger held in position and level, transfer the location of the holes to the masonry using a nail or awl. Remove the ledger board and drill 3-inch-deep anchor holes with a ⅝-inch masonry drill bit.

Drive lead anchors for a ⅜-inch lag screw into the pilot holes with a rubber mallet. Position the ledger in place and attach to the wall with ⅜-×-4-inch lag screws and washers. Tighten the lags firmly with a ratchet, being careful not to overtighten.

To prevent moisture damage to wood, apply a bead of silicon caulk in the crack between the ledger and the wall. You should also seal the lag screw heads.

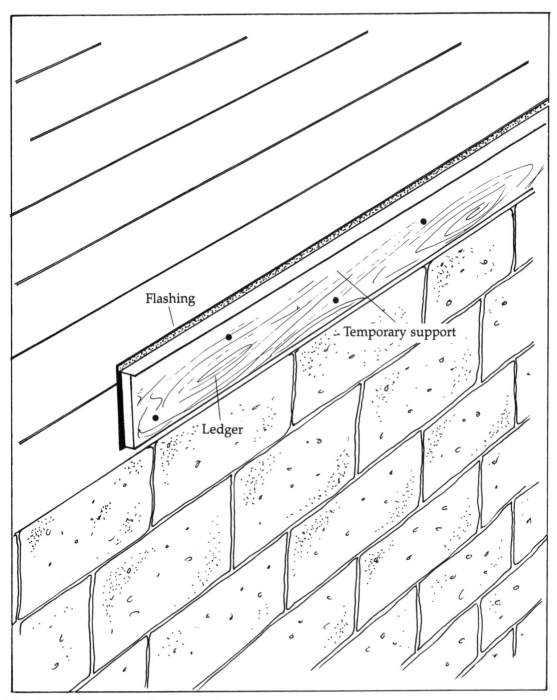

Fig. 4-11. *Ledger temporarily supported under flashing and flush to house.*

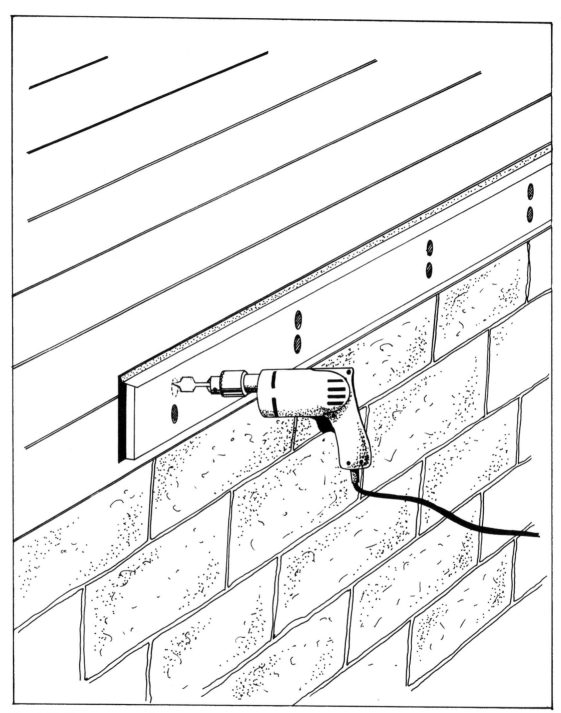

Fig. 4-12. Permanent attachment is accomplished by inserting lag bolts.

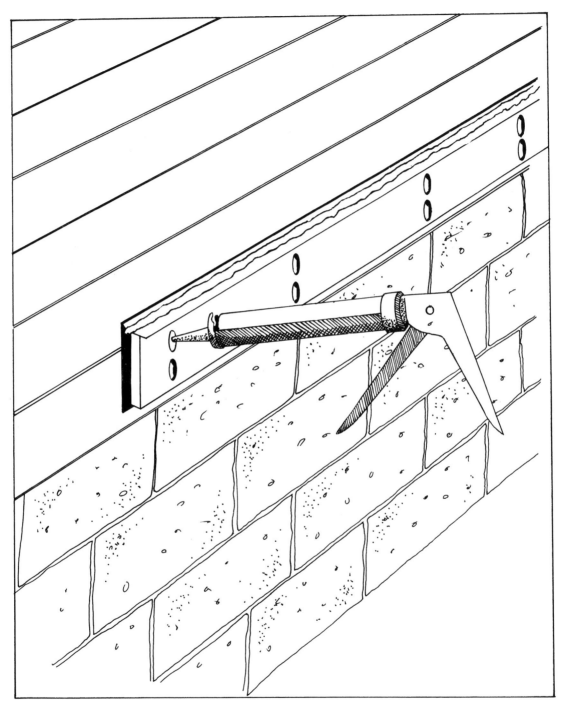

Fig. 4-13. Silicone caulk is applied to weatherproof bolts and flashing.

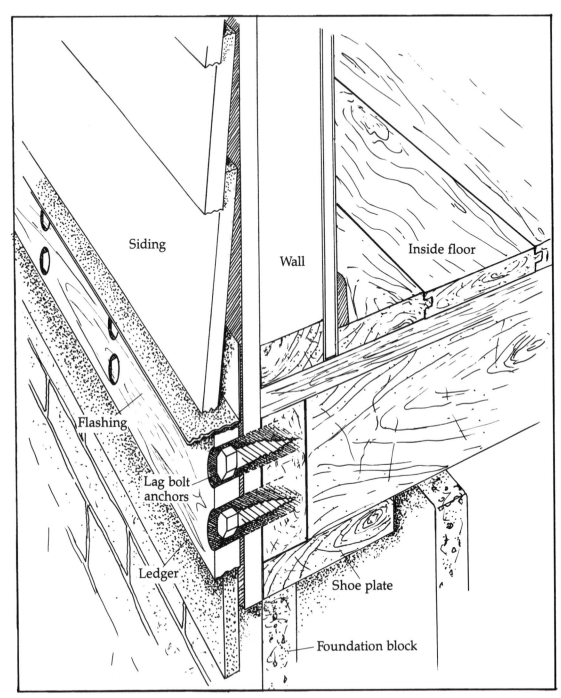

Fig. 4-14. *A cut-away view of a ledger installed on a house.*

Siding

Wall

Inside floor

Flashing

Lag bolt
anchors

Ledger

Shoe plate

Foundation block

Laying out footings

Batter boards, which resemble goal posts, are constructed of 2×4s and are used to secure mason lines for post locations. The cross piece should be about 2 feet long, and the stake is cut 10 inches longer than the post height. A point is placed on one end of each stake. Assemble the boards with the cross piece about 2 inches below the top of the stakes. Secure using 10d galvanized nails. You will need at least four batter boards.

Using your design plan as a reference, transfer measurement A (the distance from the outside edge to the post location), to the ledger board. Measure in from each end, remembering to allow for the outside joist and any facing boards. Drive a 10d nail into the bottom of the ledger at your reference mark so that a string line can be attached.

Using a sledgehammer, drive a batter board into the ground parallel to the ledger and out from the house approximately 2 feet farther than the post distance.

With the assistance of a helper, stretch a mason string from your ledger reference nail to the batter board. Drive into the ground until a line from the ledger to the top of the cross piece is level. Check using a line level. Use a carpenter square to see that the line is square (perpendicular) to the house. Wrap the line around the batter board several times to temporarily secure.

Another method to check for squareness is to measure for a right angle. Measure along the ledger and place a mark at 3 feet. Next, measure along string line and place a mark at 4 feet. An easy way to place a mark on a string line is to first mark it on a piece of masking tape and then place the tape at the proper location. In order for the line to be perpendicular, the diagonal distance between these two points should be exactly 5 feet. Adjust the string left or right until the measurement is exactly 5 feet.

Once you are sure that this line is perpendicular to the ledger, drive a 10d nail into the batter board at the string location. Leave about 1 1/2 inches exposed and tie the string to the nail; recheck level. Repeat the preceding steps to locate the other outside footing guideline.

Again, using measurements from your design, mark a point on the string line showing the distance from the house to the center of the post location. Drive batter board into the ground perpendicular to the house in line with the center of the post mark and about 2 feet outside of first guideline. This is done outside of the string line on both ends of the deck.

A third string line is then run from one batter board to the other and lined up with the marks on the first two lines. Secure this line to 10d nails so that it does not touch the other lines.

To check that all strings are square, you can compare diagonal measurements (FIG. 4-15). If the measurement of line A to D equals the measurement of B to C, the strings are square. If they differ, the third line should be adjusted until both diagonals are equal.

If any posts are to be installed between the outside posts, they must be located along the cross string. Measure from one end and place a mark along the string at the proper locations. To locate the center position of each post footing on the ground, suspend a plumb bob at the marked spots on your guide string. Drive a stake into the ground directly under the plumb bob. This procedure is repeated until all post footing locations are marked. Guidelines should be removed while digging footings, but be careful not to disturb batter board locations.

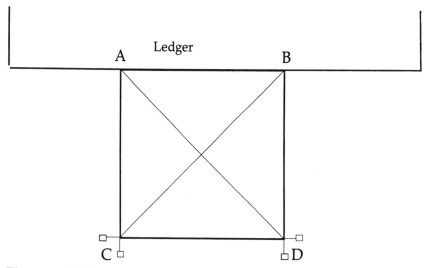

Fig. 4-15. Verify square using diagonal measures.

Pouring footings

Before you begin digging holes for footings, check with local utility providers for the location of any underground electrical, telephone, or water lines that might cross your work area. You will have to check your local codes for the depth of the footings anyway. Preshaped tube forms can be used, allowing the footings to neatly extend above ground level. Figure 4-16 indicates quantity of concrete needed for different depths and numbers of footings.

Post footing holes can be dug to a depth of 34 inches with a clam shell posthole digger (FIG. 4-17). For holes deeper than this, you will need a power auger, available from local tool rental companies.

8" Dia. Footings	Depth of Footings (Feet)			
	1'	2'	3'	4'
2	3/4	1 1/2	2 1/4	3
3	1	2 1/4	3 1/2	4 1/2
4	1 1/2	3	4 1/2	6
5	2	3 3/4	5 3/4	7 1/2

Fig. 4-16. Approximate quantity of concrete in cubic feet needed for post piers.

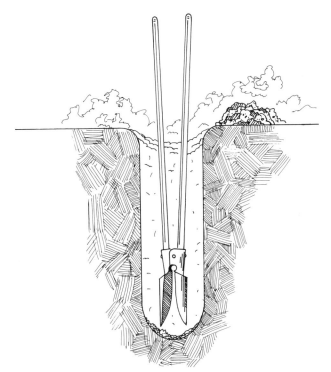

Fig. 4-17. A clamshell post hole digger makes a good hole to about 34 inches deep.

Check the depth of the hole to ensure that it conforms to local requirements. Make sure all obstacles, such as tree roots, are cut out of the hole area (FIG. 4-18). Next, fill the bottom of the hole with 2 to 3 inches of loose, coarse gravel to provide drainage under the concrete footing (FIG. 4-19).

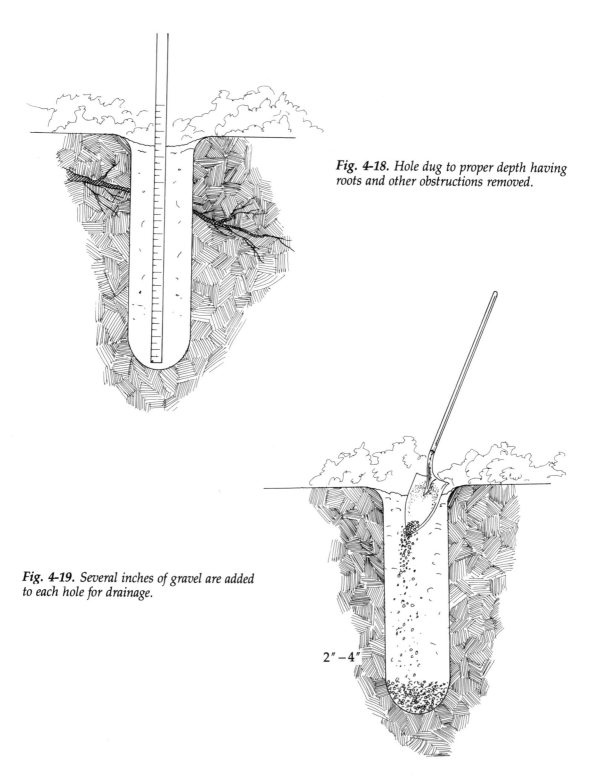

Fig. 4-18. Hole dug to proper depth having roots and other obstructions removed.

Fig. 4-19. Several inches of gravel are added to each hole for drainage.

2" – 4"

Cut concrete tube form 2 inches longer than the depth of the hole, allowing for clearance above ground level. You can cut the form using a reciprocating saw or handsaw, being careful to make the cut straight. Place the tube form into the footing hole. It should extend about 2 inches above ground level. Level the tube top with a carpenter's level, then just pack soil around the forms to hold them in place (FIG. 4-20).

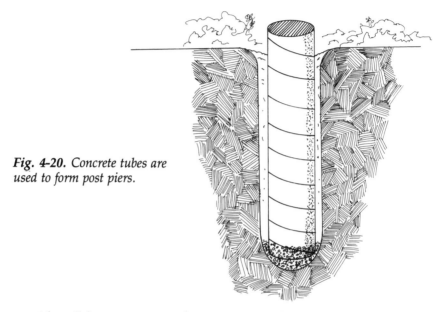

Fig. 4-20. *Concrete tubes are used to form post piers.*

After all forms are set in place, you are ready to mix the concrete. It is best to mix concrete in a wheelbarrow with a hoe (FIG. 4-21). Follow the directions provided on the bag. If you ordered ready-mixed concrete, you need only pour it into forms because it is already the correct consistency (FIG. 4-22).

Fill the forms slowly, using a long stick to tamp out any air gaps that might form in the footing. Draw a 2×4 across the top of the form in a back and forth sawing motion to level off the concrete.

After retieing your guide strings and checking all measurements, place a J-bolt in the center of each footing while the concrete is still wet. The bolts can be set in place by inserting them at an angle then wiggling to sink them into the footing. The J-bolt should extend above the concrete 3/4 to 1 inch. If any wet concrete is on the bolt threads, it must be removed at this time. A toothbrush usually works well for this purpose (FIG. 4-23A and 4-23B).

Use a plumb bob to check the location of the bolt at the center of the footing. Also, check that the J-bolt is plumb in the footing using a torpedo level (FIG. 4-24A, FIG. 4-24B, and FIG. 4-24C). Allow concrete to cure completely, then remove the exposed tube form with a utility knife.

Fig. 4-21. Tools needed to mix concrete include a wheelbarrow, concrete, hoe, fresh mix, and clean water.

Fig. 4-22. Backfilling tube, making sure it is well packed.

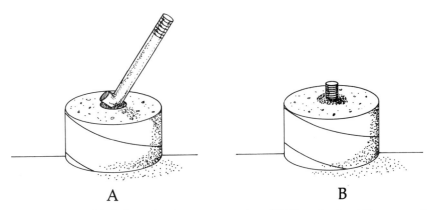

A   B

Fig. 4-23. A) J-bolt insertion in wet concrete.   B) Threads should be exposed and clean.

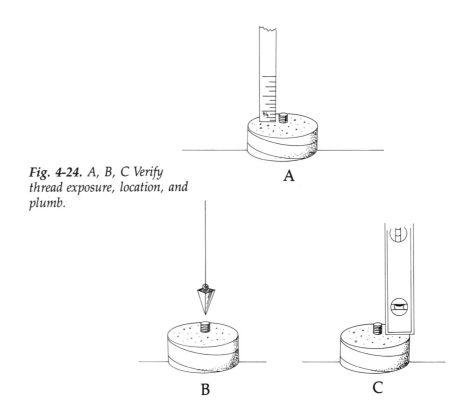

Fig. 4-24. A, B, C Verify thread exposure, location, and plumb.

A

B   C

Post anchors are installed on footings so that they are parallel to the ledger (FIG. 4-25). This is done by laying a 2×4 across several footings and parallel to the ledger. Draw a reference line along the 2×4 on top of each footing. Locate the post anchor over the J-bolt and square to the refer-

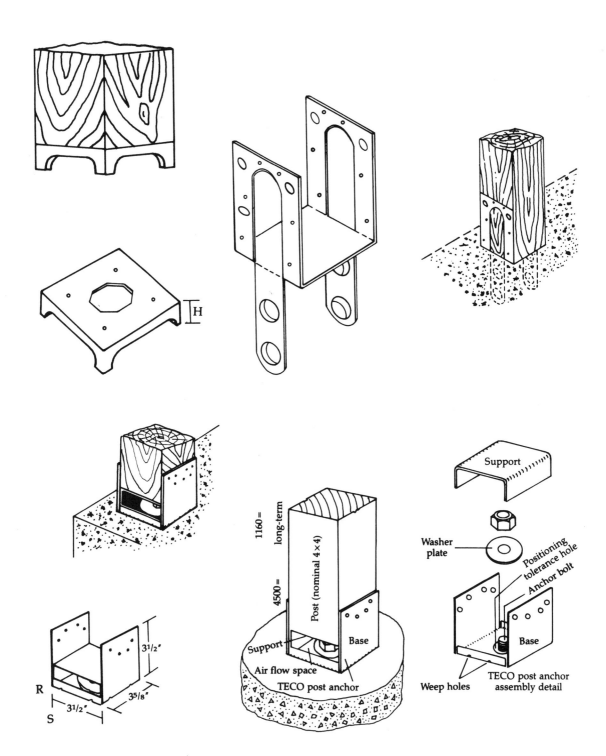

Fig. 4-25. *Typical post anchors.* Compliments of TECO-Lumber-LOK.

ence line. Each anchor is then secured with a nut on the J-bolt. Be sure that the anchor remains centered and square to the reference line.

Cut posts to length, as determined in your design, plus a margin of 6 inches. The extra length will allow you to cut the posts exactly to the proper height when anchored in place.

Set posts in the anchor and temporarily secure them with a 6d galvanized nail. Attach a 1-×-4 brace midpoint of the post and extend diagonally to the ground. Drive a 2-×-2 stake in the ground near the end of the brace. These braces hold posts plumb and should be attached to two sides of each post.

Check the plumb of each post with a level. When plumb is obtained, firmly attach the brace to the ground stake so that the post will not move. Repeat this on both sides of all stakes. Once the posts are plumb and braced, you can now permanently secure them to the anchors using 6d galvanized nails on all sides.

The exact height of all posts can now be measured. Using a long, straight 2×4, place one end on the top edge of the ledger. The free end should rest against the face of a post. Level the post with a carpenter's level. Place a pencil mark on the post beneath the bottom edge of the 2×4. In corner post construction, this line indicates the top of the beam; in cantilevered construction, it represents the top of the joists. This difference is explained in the following section. Repeat the preceding last two steps for all outside post heights.

Beam location

When measuring and installing beams, it is important to understand whether your deck will be cantilevered construction or corner-post construction. A cantilevered deck is one in which the posts and beams are set in from the edge of the deck. To accomplish this, the joists must run across the beam. Many feel that this type of construction gives a neater, more attractive finished look. A cantilevered portion of a deck should be no more than 1/3 the total length of the joist.

Corner-post deck construction differs in that the posts are positioned at the edges of the deck. This causes joists to butt flush to the beam as opposed to setting on the beam. This type of construction is ideal for low decks when height restricts the ability to stack joists on beams. Not only is the joist position different between these two types of constructions, but also the method of beam attachment. Both methods are covered in the following sections.

Cantilevered deck construction

Your deck design will determine the length of beams. In cantilevered construction, the length of the beam matches the exact width of the deck. Measure two pressure-treated boards to this length and cut them square using a circular saw.

Set the two beams together and mark the locations of the posts. After measuring the positions, use a combination square to mark the tops and faces of the beam boards.

With the help of an assistant, place one beam on the inside of the posts parallel to the ledger. Tack in place using 12d galvanized nails. Remember to locate the beam lower than your pencil mark by the width of the joist board. The top of the joist, not the top of the beam, needs to be level with the top of the ledger.

Drill $1/4$-inch pilot holes through the beam into the post and counter-bore a $1/2$-inch-deep hole using a 1-inch spade bit. The holes should be in pairs in each post.

Using a ratchet, secure the beam to posts using $3/8$-$\times$-4-inch lag screws and washers. Seal lag screw heads with silicon caulking. Repeat to attach the other beam to the opposite (outside) face of the post. Using a reciprocating saw or handsaw, cut the top of the posts so that they are flush with the top of the beam.

Corner-post deck construction

The length of the beams in corner-post construction differs from canti-lever construction in the manner in which they are attached to posts. First, measure and cut a board to a length equal to the distance from the outside edges of each outside post. Cut the second beam board 3 inches longer than the first board. This allows the outside joist on each end to be attached to the outside of the post and butt into the inside face of the second beam board.

Set the shorter beam in place on the outside of the posts parallel to the ledger. Align the top edge of the beam with your pencil mark so that it is level with the top of the ledger. Tack in place using 12d galvanized nails.

Set the second longer board against the outside of the other board with the top edges flush. The ends of the long board should extend $1^1/2$ inches over both ends of the short board. Tack in place using 12d galva-nized nails. Nail the beams together using 16d galvanized nails ran-domly placed.

Drill $1/4$-inch pilot holes through the beam into the post and counter-bore $1/2$-inch-deep holes using a 1-inch spade bit. The holes should be in pairs in each post.

Using a ratchet, secure beam to posts, using $3/8$-$\times$-5-inch lag screws and washers. Seal lag screw heads with silicon caulking.

Outside joist placement

At this stage in your construction, you have set your posts and secured the beams. You are now ready to cut and attach joists, which are the main support for your decking boards.

Cantilevered deck construction

Refer to your design plan for the appropriate length and spacing of joists. Remember that the joist can overhang only $1/3$ the total length of the joist. Measure all joists to the proper length and mark a guideline using a combination square. Cut the joists along the guideline with a circular saw.

Place the outside joist on top of the beam and attach one end to the ledger with 16d galvanized nails. Secure the outside joist to the beam by toenailing with a 12d galvanized nail. Attach the other outside joist to the opposite end of the deck.

The header joist is now cut to equal the width of the deck. Mark this length using a combination square then carefully cut it with a circular saw. Line up the header joist with the outside joist, making sure all edges are flush. Secure the header joist using 16d galvanized nails.

A metal angle bracket can be added to provide additional strength in each corner. These premanufactured metal fasteners can be found at your local lumberyard. Refer to the section on fasteners in chapter 1 for additional information.

Corner-post deck construction

Measure the distance from the ledger to the beam on the outside of each corner post. Use this length to cut two outside joists. Place outside joist against the post flush with the end of the beam and flush with the ledger at the other end. Secure the ledger end of the joist using 16d galvanized nails. Tack the post end of the joist using 10d galvanized nails.

Drill a $1/4$-inch pilot hole through the joist into the beam and counterbore pilot holes $1/2$ inch deep using a 1-inch spade bit. With a ratchet, secure the joist to the beam using a $3/8$-$\times$-4-inch lag screw and washer. So that lag screws can be installed more easily, run the threads of the lag screws across a bar of soap.

Using a reciprocating saw or a handsaw, cut the top of the posts so that they are flush with the top of the beam.

Inside joist placement

Before you begin installing joists, refer to your design plan for the joist spacing. Measure along the ledger from the outside edge of your outside joist and mark the location of the inside joists. Draw a reference line at each location using a combination square.

Measure along the beam from the same outside edge, and mark the location of the inside joists. Draw a reference line at each location using a combination square. If this is cantilevered construction, you will also need to transfer the joist locations to the header joist.

Attach premanufactured joist hangers to the ledger and header joist using 10d galvanized nails (FIG. 4-26). Be sure that one of the flanges is flush against the reference line.

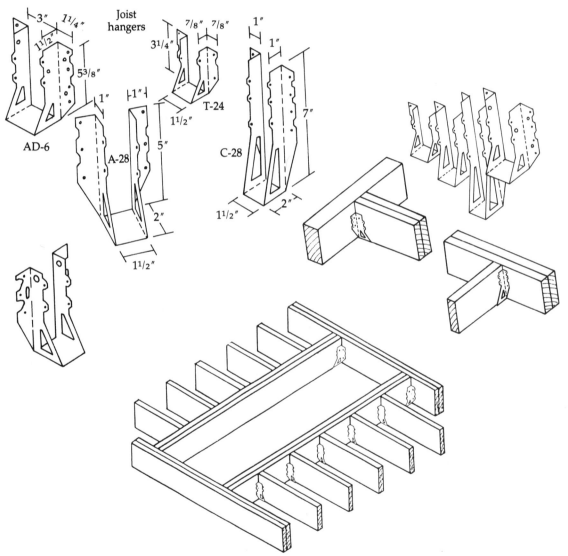

Fig. 4-26. *Typical premanufactured joist hangers.* Compliments of TECO-Lumber-LOK.

Use a cut-off scrap from a joist board as a template to secure the other flange of each joist hanger. Place the scrap in the joist hanger, bringing the loose flange flush against the joist. Secure using 10d galvanized nails and remove scrap template. Do this for all joist hangers on the ledger and header joist. Carefully measure, mark, and cut all joists to the proper length. Taking your time will help ensure neat, square cuts.

Set the joist into the joist hangers, being careful that the flashing rests on top of the joist at the ledger. The joist should be set with the crown side up. Using 10d galvanized nails, secure each joist hanger to both sides of each joist.

If the joists are cantilevered, they will rest on top of the beam and be secured. This is accomplished by toenailing from each side of the joist into the beam using 10d galvanized nails.

The header joist is secured to the end of each joist by driving 16d galvanized nails through the header into the end of each joist. A nail placed at the top and bottom of the joist helps to prevent the joist from twisting (FIGS. 4-27 and 4-28).

Fig. 4-27. Structural members for two deck levels in place.

Deck boards

When possible, it is best to purchase deck boards that are long enough to span the entire width of the deck. If your pattern or deck size makes this

Fig. 4-28. Beam is positioned to carry the load of the upper and lower decks.

impractical, always butt ends over solid support and stagger joints from row to row (FIGS. 4-29 and 4-30).

Place the first row of the deck boards in position against the house and over the flashing. This board should be cut to the correct length because trimming after installation will be difficult next to the house. Make sure that the first board is set square on the deck. Secure using the proper nails. Nails used to secure deck boards will be sized according to board thickness. Deck boards that are 5/4 inch can be secured using 7d galvanized nails while 10d galvanized nails would be used for 2-×-6 or 2-×-8 deck boards.

Set the remaining deck boards in place so that one edge is flush to an outside joist and the other end overhangs. The overhang will be removed later after all deck boards have been secured. When laying the boards in place, make sure that the bark side is down. Boards tend to cup toward the bark side, and facing this cup down keeps water from catching and laying on the deck.

Using a 16d galvanized nail as a spacer, push each successive row against the previously secured deck board. Attach the deck board to each joist with a pair of nails. Angling the nails toward each other improves the holding power. Remove the spacer nails and move on to the next row.

Wood Type	Maximum Allowable Span (inches)			
	Laid Flat		Laid On Edge	
	5/4 x 6	2 x 4	2 x 3	2 x 4
Southern Pine	24	60	90	144
Cedar or Redwood	20	42	66	108

Fig. 4-29. Deck board spans.

Fig. 4-30. Pneumatic nailer eases deck board installation.

After you have nailed approximately half of the deck boards in place, measure the remaining joist space. If the space will not allow deck boards to end flush with the end of the deck, the spacing must be adjusted. A change in row gaps will be less noticeable if it is done a little bit at a time over a number of rows. Sometimes, instead of adjusting the gap, each row might need to be made smaller to accommodate the space. If downsizing the width of a row is necessary, do it gradually over many rows, as was done with the gap spacing.

When all deck boards are in place, it is time to trim off the overhang.

Mark the outside edge of the outside joist on your deck boards with a chalk line. Set the depth of your circular saw to just a little deeper (about 1/8 inch) than the thickness of the deck boards. Cut the overhang along the chalk line. If there are areas that cannot be reached with the circular saw, you will have to remove the overhanging pieces with a handsaw.

If your design calls for face boards, cut and measure them then attach them to the deck using 10d galvanized nails. Make sure that the top surfaces are flush.

Stairs

To build a proper set of stairs, you need to calculate the number of steps, the rise, the tread, and the span (FIG. 4-31). The number of steps depends on the vertical drop or the distance from the top of the deck to the ground. To calculate the number of steps, measure the vertical drop and divide by 7. Uneven divisions should be rounded off to the nearest whole number. For example, if the vertical drop equals 36 inches when divided by 7 it will equal 5.14 inches. Rounding off makes the number of steps 5.

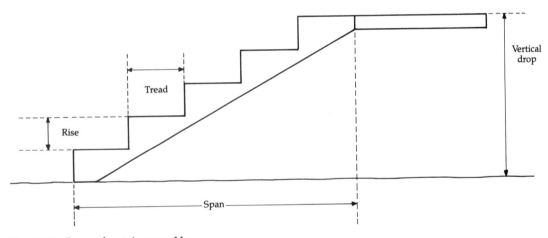

Fig. 4-31. Parts of a stair assembly.

The next measurement to calculate is the rise. The rise is the vertical distance between treads and is found by dividing the vertical drop by the number of steps. A rise of approximately 7 inches is a measurement most recommended by local building codes. In our previous example, the vertical drop of 36 inches divided by 5 steps equals a rise of 7.2 inches.

The tread (width of step) is usually constructed from a pair of 2×6s yielding a width of 11 1/4 inches. If you choose other lumber to construct the tread, the distance is found by actually measuring the depth of the tread plus any spacing between boards.

The final measurement calculated for stairs is the span. The span of the stairway tells you how far from the deck the stairs will end. This measurement will locate the distance horizontally from the deck to set your support posts. The posts should be set 18 inches short of the total span distance. The span is calculated by multiplying the number of treads times the tread width. In our example, the tread width is 11$1/4$ inches with 4 treads (the number of treads is always one less than the number of steps). Therefore, the span will be 45 inches and the support posts will be located 27 inches out from the deck.

Using your design plan, locate your stairs on your deck. Measure and mark the location of the stair stringers on the side of the deck. Lay a long, straight 2×4 on top of your deck over the stringer location so that it is square to the deck and level. Suspend a plumb bob from this 2×4 the distance from your deck as calculated earlier for stair post location.

Using a post hole digger, dig your hole, pour post footings, and attach metal post anchors to the footing. Secure 4-×-4 posts to metal anchors.

Set the stringer on sawhorses and mark the rise and tread measurements on each stringer. This is done using a framing square. One leg of the square is marked with masking tape for the length of the tread and the other leg is marked to show the rise. Starting at one end of the stringer, position the framing square so that the taped marks are both flush to the edge of the board. Draw a pencil line along the edge of the square. Continue this for all steps starting at the end of each previous step outline. Each end of the stringer will need to be trimmed along the guidelines with a circular saw.

Using a piece of scrap stair tread, mark this thickness along the bottom of each tread line on your stringer. Premanufactured metal tread cleats are attached to each stringer using $1/4$-×-1$1/4$-inch lag screws. It is best to drill $1/8$-inch pilot holes for each lag screw. Position the cleats flush with the bottom of each tread outline.

Attach the stringers to the deck using premanufactured metal angle brackets, which are first secured to the stringer using 5d galvanized nails. The angle brackets should be flush with the cut ends of the stringers. Hold the stringers in place and secure to the edge of the deck using 8d galvanized nails.

Pilot holes are drilled $1/4$ inch through the stringer into each post. Each pilot hole is then countersunk $1/2$ inch deep using a 1-inch spade bit. Secure the stringer to the post with $3/8$-×-4-inch lag screws and washers. Seal lag head holes with silicone caulk.

Once stringers are securely attached, remeasure the width of the stair treads. Cut two 2-×-6 boards for each tread—a standard tread width. Place the front 2×6 of each step on the metal cleat so that the front edge of the tread board is flush with the edge of the stringer. Drill

1/8-inch pilot holes through the cleat. Secure with a 1/4- × -1¼-inch lag screw. Place the second tread board on the cleat allowing for a small gap between it and the front board. A 16d nail works as a good spacer. Secure the second board as you did the first. Repeat this procedure for all the steps in your stairway.

An alternate method for tread attachment would be to nail treads directly to a notched stringer. You would lay the stringers out the same way with your framing square, but instead of attaching cleats, you would use your circular saw to remove the wood in the step area.

Railings

The finishing touch to any deck construction is the installation of railings. Most local codes require a deck rail of at least 34 inches above the decking and spindle spacing less than 6 inches. Make sure you check your local building codes.

The location of your railing posts should be identified on your design plan. If you forgot this stage of the design, don't panic. Posts should be set at the head of the stairs on each side and at all corners. When spacing the interior posts, split the distance from corners or stair posts in even units so that the space will always be less than 6 feet.

Measure and cut to length all 4- × -4 railing posts using a circular saw or, if available, a power miter box. The total length of the post will be the height above the deck boards less rail thickness, as required by code, plus the thickness of the joist and deck board. Posts are cut square at the top and the bottoms are usually finished off with a 45° angle.

Drill 1/4-inch pilot holes at the bottom of each post approximately 4 inches apart. Each pilot hole should then be counter-bored 1/2 inch using a 1-inch spade bit. Place posts in position on deck joists and mark the location of the pilot holes. Care must be taken that posts are set plumb as checked with your level. Set posts aside and drill 1/4-inch pilot holes in deck joists. Attach posts with 3/8- × -4-inch lag screws and washers using your ratchet.

Measure and cut 2- × -4 side rails. If you must have a joint, it has to fall at a post so that each end can be fastened securely. Cutting each end at a 45° angle and overlapping results in a stronger and more attractive joint. Side rails are positioned with edges flush to the top of the post and attached to the inside of each post using a 2½-inch galvanized deck screw. With end grains at joints, splits can be avoided if 1/16-inch pilot holes are predrilled. Check that the side rail is level and adjust it if needed. It is always better to check and adjust level at stages than see the mistake in a finished project.

Measure the height of the railing post at the stairway and transfer this distance to each bottom post on the stair stringers. The measurement is taken from the top edge of the stringer on the high side of the post.

With the help of an assistant, position a 2×4 on stairway posts. The 2×4s should be set to the inside of each post. The top edge is aligned with the top rear corner of the top post and the pencil mark on the lower post. Mark the outline of the upper post and rail on the stairway rail. Also mark the outline of the stairway rail on the lower post. The rail extends beyond the bottom post a distance equal to the extension of the stringer.

At this point, a plumb line is marked using your level while the 2×4 is still held in place. These marks will be your guide when cutting the 2×4 with a circular saw. The mark on the side of the post should be extended completely around the post using a combination square. Remove the top of the post by cutting carefully along this line with a reciprocating saw or handsaw. The side rail is then attached permanently to the stair posts using 2¹/2-inch galvanized deck screws.

Measure and cut the 2-×-6 cap board. Corners are mitered at a 45° angle for a more finished appearance. Attach the cap board using 2¹/2-inch galvanized deck screws so that the inside edges are flush. The screws are also used to secure the cap board to each post. The cap board on the stairway rail is attached the same way except after the spindles are attached. The stairway cap board is cut to the same length as the side rail board and is bevel-cut at the top to fit around the top post.

Measure and cut to length all 2-×-2 spindles except stairway spindles. The length of the spindle should be 1 inch shorter than the length of the railing post. Cut off spindles square on top and with a 45° angle on the bottom. Cuts can be made more accurately with a power miter box, although a circular saw can produce satisfactory results.

Starting at a corner post or stairway post, position spindles using a spacer block. The spacer block is cut from scrap lumber and should measure less than 6 inches wide. The spindle should be set flush against the bottom of the cap board. The bottom of the spindle is set tight against the spacer and attached using a 2¹/2-inch galvanized deck screw. Using your level, plumb the spindle then attach it to the side rail using a 2¹/2-inch galvanized deck screw. An additional 2¹/2-inch galvanized deck screw is placed in the top and bottom of each spindle, making the installation complete. Predrilling 1/8-inch pilot holes in the spindle helps prevent splitting. This procedure is repeated for all spindles on the deck.

Place the spindles on the stairway so that the bottom is flush with the bottom of the stringer. Draw a pencil mark along the top of the side rail on the spindle. Cut the spindle at this mark with a circular saw. Repeat this procedure for all spindles in the stairway. Stair spindles are attached using 2¹/2-inch galvanized deck screws in the same fashion as the deck spindles.

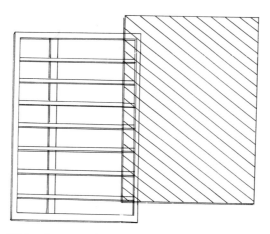

Wider framing for support

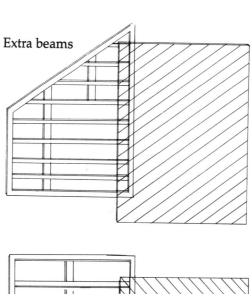

Extra beams

Doubled
joists to
support
pattern

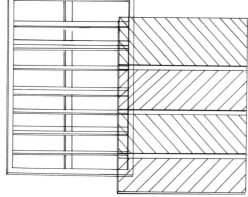

Fig. 4-32. Framing requirements for special deck patterns.

Finish off the construction of your railing by attaching the cap board to the stairway side rail using 2¹/₂-inch galvanized deck screws.

Now it is time to Relax! Step back and enjoy your work! If your deck design used alternate deck board patterns, it will be necessary to supplement deck bracing with additional joists or beams (FIG. 4-32).

Sample materials list

The following is a materials list for a 10-×-12-foot deck, 30 inches above grade with a 34-inch railing.

Flashing: 12′×12″
Deck posts: 3, 4″×4″×26″ or 1   10′ piece
Deck post anchors: 3
Ledger board: 1, 2×8×12′
Beams: 2, 2×8×12′
Joists: 11, 2×8×10′
Joist hangers: 9
Header board: 1, 2×8×12′
³/₈″×4″ lag screws and washers: 24 each
Silicone caulk: 1 tube
Nails box (decking): 10# 16d, 10# 12d, 10# 8d, and 10# 7d
Stair stringers: 2, 2×12×40″ or 1, 10′ piece
2-×-4 side rails: 4, 12″
2×6 cap board: 4, 12′
4×4 railing posts: 8, 3′
2×6 stair treads: 6, 3′
Tread cleats: 12
Deck boards: 24, ⁵/₄″×6″×12′
Spindles: 80, 2″×2″×42″
Concrete footing forms: 5 lengths
J-bolts: 5
Concrete: enough for 5 footings
Joist angle (corner): 2

Decorative fencing provides a surface for training vines and shrubs.

Premanufactured stone blocks interlock to form a smoothly curved wall.

Erosion problems on a steep grade are solved with terraced retaining walls.

Yard separation is accomplished rustically with a stacked split-rail fence (no posts are needed).

A stone planter harmonizes well with the bricks on the walkway and steps.

The theme of climbing vines on the fence and lamppost is reinforced with window boxes.

Simple fencing adds a touch of accent for a perennial garden.

A gently curving walkway and well-prepared, low-maintenance beds are a pleasing invitation to homeowner and visitor.

Add interest to a walkway by incorporating a stream and footbridge.

Gazebos provide a pleasant shelter regardless of the weather.

Trellises and arbors are easily and pleasantly accented with colorful vines and annuals.

Susan Riley

Planter boxes built as an extension of the house's architecture.

The relaxing atmosphere of water can easily be added to your landscape with a simple (or complex) reflecting pool.

A stone wall along a patio area provides a seat for your favorite plants.

Jorge L. Figueroa Alvarado
Calle 23, YY-19, Sta. Juanita
Bayamón, PR 00956
802-35-3456

5

Walkways and steps

The main function of paving, to provide a hard surface, is not its only function. Paving also provides a sense of direction, leading people to areas that might not otherwise be obvious; provides an area of repose; reinforces the character of a particular setting; or provides a sheltered niche in a garden corner or under a tree where visitors can stop to gaze, chat, or spend time in solitude. The type of paving, its pattern and edging, all have an enormous effect on the mood or character of a particular surrounding.

A walkway should be functional but it can also transport you from point A to point B in a graceful, relaxing fashion. Location of walkways, such as front entrances and service entrances, are easily determined. Walkway routes are sometimes best laid out by walking through your garden. Take note of the special features in your yard that you might want to visit on a regular basis. While the shortest distance between two points is a straight line, a garden path usually feels more comfortable if it meanders or curves, revealing special delights along its length.

The walkway to a front door needs to accommodate a number of people at one time but allow for comfortable, safe, and easy access. To avoid confusion with secondary or service walkways, the primary entry must be designed and planted with importance. This detail allows you not only to identify the front door, but also conveys a feeling of welcome. Major walkways are most comfortable at 4 to 5 feet wide, while casual or secondary walkways can be about 3 feet wide.

Materials used for walkways include bricks, cobblestone, flagstone, slate, interlocking paving blocks, and gravel. No matter the material, the finished surface should be safe, even, and comfortable.

Designing your walkway

Always design your project before construction. This is a fun and vital step towards a project that is well built and fits into your garden aesthetically. The first task of designing your walkway is to sketch your home and property to an appropriate scale on graph paper (see Appendix G). Usually, this is represented by a certain distance on the paper ($^1/_4$ inch) which is equal to a certain actual distance (4 feet) on the ground in your garden. Locate as accurately as possible, all features that might affect, or be affected by, your project. This would include such items as driveways, existing walkways, front entrances, side entrances, patios, and clotheslines. Any additional buildings on your property, like garages, toolsheds, or pool cabanas, must also be included on your sketch. Lay tracing paper over your design so that you can sketch your walkway ideas without altering your property sketch.

Laying out your project

When you are comfortable with what you have on paper, go outside in your garden. Using string lines and stakes, transfer your paper ideas to the ground. If you designed a curved walkway, a garden hose is helpful in laying out the project. Look at what you have on the ground from several areas. Walk along the proposed walkway. If it satisfies all your needs, continue by estimating your project's materials.

Estimating materials

Your final design should now be sketched on graph paper and its size can be easily calculated. When you started the sketch, it was necessary to determine an appropriate scale. Measure the size of your proposed walkway, counting all the $^1/_4$-inch increments and multiply by 4 (using the preceding example). A measurement of $1^1/_4$ inches equals 5, $^1/_4$-inch increments and represents a total actual ground distance of 20 feet (5 units $\times$ 4 feet = 20 feet).

Your plan will provide you with measurements in only two dimensions—length and width. The length is important in calculating how much edge material, i.e., railroad ties, is needed, and when multiplied by the width, gives you the total square feet of surface material needed. A walkway 20 feet long and 5 feet wide will need 40 feet of edging material, 2 edges of 20 feet each, and 100 square feet of surface material, 20 feet $\times$ 5 feet.

Before you can begin estimating the quantity of material you'll need, you have to decide on the type of paving that will be used on your walkway. Some suppliers might be able to tell you the number of pieces of a particular material you'll need to cover a 1-square-foot area.

A rule of thumb when using a standard paving brick is that five bricks are needed to cover a 1-square-foot area. This allows for most patterns and the need to cut some bricks. If you are using a wild pattern or irregular material, it is easy to determine your own piece count. Measure a box on the ground 2×2 feet and place your surface material into this grid. Set the material using the desired pattern. Count the number of pieces of material used in this 4-square-foot area (2×2 feet = 4 square feet). To find the average number of pieces per square foot, divide the total number of pieces in your grid by 4, rounding to the next highest whole piece. A 4-square-foot grid containing 25 pieces would be equivalent to 7 pieces per square foot.

Once you know the number of pieces per square foot and the total square feet of surface area to cover, you can calculate the total number of pieces of surface material needed to complete your walkway project.

Keep in mind that, when working with brick, slate, or other materials that need to be cut, some breakage and waste can be expected. Therefore, add an additional 5 percent to the total number of pieces to help offset waste. It is better to have a little extra left at the end of the job than to need just a few pieces to finish. Following our example, you would need to order 525 bricks:

$$100 \text{ ft}^2 \text{ area} \times 5 \text{ bricks/ft}^2 = 500 \text{ bricks} + 5\%$$

The other materials you will need to estimate are the gravel and sand that will be used as a base. A few more basic calculations will give you these quantities. A quarry or stone yard sells these materials by weight or, in some cases, by volume. It is important that you check which method of measurement is used by your local supplier.

Our sample walkway of 100 feet in length and 5 feet in width needs to have a 6-inch base of coarse gravel and a 2-inch base of sand. The volume of each of these is expressed in cubic feet or cubic yards. A cubic foot is an area 1 foot wide by 1 foot long by 1 foot deep, and a cubic yard is an area $3 \times 3 \times 3$ containing 27 cubic feet.

The coarse gravel needed is 250 cubic feet, 5 feet wide $\times$ 100 feet long $\times$ 0.5 deep. The 250 cubic feet can be expressed as $9^{1}/_{4}$ cubic yards by dividing by 27. The sand is found in the same way, remembering that the depth is only a part of a whole foot. In this case, it is 2 inches or 0.166 feet. The calculation reads $5 \times 100 \times 0.166$ and equals 83.3 cubic feet, or 3.08 cubic yards (83.3/27).

If your supplier measures quantity by weight, you'll need to know how much 1 cubic yard of material weighs. The supplier will be able to give you this information. If 1 cubic yard of sand weighs 1 ton, you would need 3.08 tons of sand for this project. A ton of anything equals 2,000 pounds, so unless you have a large truck, most of these bulk materials will need to be delivered.

The final calculation is to determine the cost for all these materials. Call your supplier and tell him what you need and he will quote a price for each material. In this sample project, we know that we need 525 bricks, 9 1/4 cubic yards of coarse gravel, 3.08 cubic yards of sand, and 40 feet of edging material. Before you order all your materials, however, you'll need to prepare the work area and provide an area for materials to be stored when delivered.

Assembling tools

Many of the tools you'll need for this project might already be in your garage (see FIG. 5-1). Appendix A is a chart listing tools that you might need to complete the job. By checking off the appropriate column in the chart, you will have a clear idea of the tools that you own or those that you will need to rent or buy.

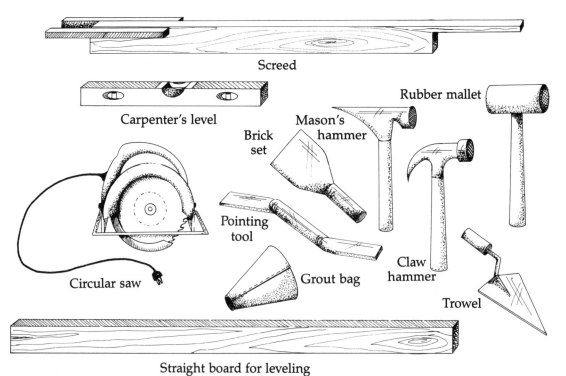

Screed

Carpenter's level

Brick set

Mason's hammer

Rubber mallet

Circular saw

Pointing tool

Grout bag

Claw hammer

Trowel

Straight board for leveling

Fig. 5-1. Useful tools in constructing most walkway projects.

Step-by-step construction

Regardless of the surface material you have chosen, five basic steps are common to constructing walkways:

1. Excavating.
2. Forming.
3. Laying a subbase.
4. Installing footings, water pipes, and electric wires.
5. Presoaking.

Follow these five steps first, which are covered in the following sections, then refer to the section that explains the finishing steps for specific surface materials, such as concrete or brick.

Excavation

If the existing grade is flush (at the same level) with the proposed walkway surface, soil will need to be excavated to allow for a subbase of stone and sand. If the existing grade is lower than the desired grade, however, backfill will be needed for the subbase and surface material. If fill is used, it needs to be retained and thoroughly compacted before a surface material is added.

When installing any paved area, it is important to remember proper drainage. Grading should be done so that any water running off the paved area will flow away from the house or other building foundation and towards a dispersal area. Runoff should be dispersed over as large an area as possible to avoid possible problems associated with collection all in one location. Always set pitch using a carpenter's level on a straight board, a line level, or a surveyor's level (FIG. 5-2). Sighting by eye can prove disastrous, because slopes can be very deceiving to most eyes. A rule of thumb for pitch away from a foundation is a 1-inch drop in elevation for every 10 feet of walkway.

Forming

Forming is important in concrete work because it defines the final shape of the project. While most forms usually stay in place and become a permanent part of the walkway, concrete forms are usually removed after concrete has cured.

If the framing is an integral part of the design, it needs to be of a permanent nature. Redwood or cedar are naturally long-lasting, while other wood types can be treated to provide permanency. When setting the forms in place, remember that the top surface of the form needs to be flush (level) with the finished surface of the walkway. This allows for proper installation and a neat appearance to the finished project.

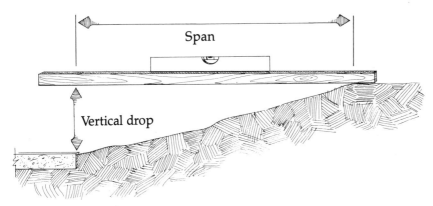

Fig. 5-2. Change in elevation is measured with a straight board and carpenter's level.

Laying a subbase

A subbase provides an excellent cushion for minimizing the effects of heaving. It also provides a solid base, or foundation, for any surface material, regardless of weather extremes. Check your local codes because subbases are often **required**, not just recommended. Even in areas where it is not a requirement, it is still a good idea (FIG. 5-3).

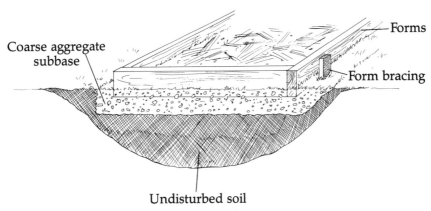

Fig. 5-3. Typical subbase preparation for walkway projects.

A subbase is generally a 4- to 6-inch layer of coarse gravel. If your area is subject to extreme weather, it is better to have a thicker subbase. Repairing a walkway that has heaved due to freezing and thawing is more trouble than spending a little extra time and money on the original subbase.

Place stone in the excavated area and tamp for compaction every 2 inches of fill. If your project is extensive, look into leasing a power tamper. This very helpful tool might well be worth the expense and is commonly available through equipment rental stores.

A 2-inch layer of sand is filled in on top of the compacted subbase, which is also compacted for brick or flagstone finishes. This layer is a leveling layer and allows you to adjust for minor differences in thicknesses of your surfacing material (FIG. 5-4).

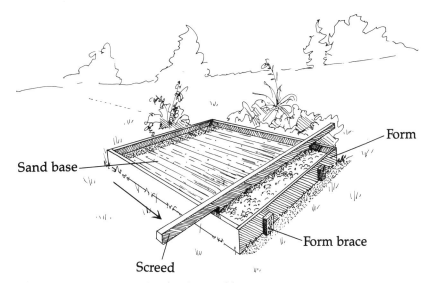

Fig. 5-4. A screed is used to level a sand base.

Installing footings, water pipes, and electric wires

If you plan to have lights along your walkway, you'll need to rough in the wires before completing your project (FIG. 5-5). Chapter 10 covers lighting and lighting design in detail. Anything else that might require a portion of the walkway to be removed should be completed prior to finishing the walkway. It is always easier to dig a trench for a water line or electric wires before the walkway creates an obstruction.

When a trellis or arbor is to be installed, the footings should be dug and poured, allowing your surface pattern to be laid, without disturbing, for a later project.

Presoaking

After soil is well compacted, it should be uniformly moistened. This step is very important when pouring concrete. If the soil is dry, it will draw moisture out of the concrete mix and the finish might become splotchy when it cures. The forms should also be wet to prevent any curing problems.

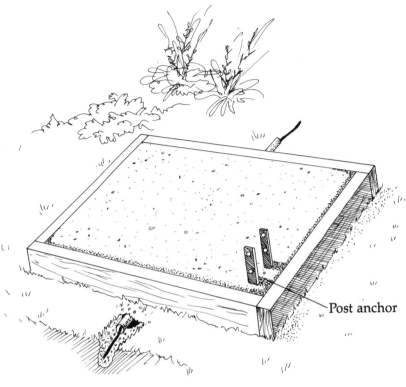

Post anchor

Wire installed in pipe

Fig. 5-5. Wires and post anchor hardware need to be incorporated before project is complete.

Concrete walkways

Although concrete is a practical, durable surface choice, it is not always the first choice for aesthetics. The problems of appearance have been overcome recently through a wide range of textures, colors, and layouts as well as molds for stamping out patterns. Most of these options are available to the do-it-yourselfer. Still, there is the labor-intensive nature of concrete.

Concrete work requires some bull work. If the thought of the extra physical labor or finishing the slab frightens you, seek the advice of a professional. In many cases, you might be able to be the general contractor. This means that you design the project, set up the forms, and grade. You then call in a commercial company to subcontract the pouring and finish the project.

Control joints

Expansion needs to be allowed to minimize the possibility of cracking. If a crack does occur, it will not destroy the entire project. Only the portion of walkway between the control joints need be repaired. Expansion or control joints must be provided for slab areas greater than 200 square feet or narrow areas (walkways) more than 50 square feet. This rule of thumb is only general, check local codes first so that you conform to your area's requirements. Felt or fiber strips are typical expansion joints, but redwood, cedar, or vinyl can be used for a more attractive joint.

Reinforcement

Reinforcement is an additional measure used to minimize the possibility of cracking on unstable ground or on areas that will have heavy vehicular traffic. Typically, $1/2$-inch reinforcing rods are placed 24 inches on center in both directions and secured at the intersections with wire. Another type of reinforcing is welded mesh wire with 6-×-6-inch square grids. In order to locate reinforcing mesh in the middle of a slab, it must be held off the ground during pouring. This is done by laying a brick under several grid intersections. If the pour is more than 4 inches deep, something other than a 2-inch-thick brick will be needed to get the reinforcing material into the middle of the slab.

Mixing

If you are doing a small area (1 cubic yard or less) you will be able to mix the concrete in a large wheelbarrow. When working with concrete, it is important to know the quantity that you'll need, and it is especially important if you are ordering premixed concrete, because you must be able to tell your supplier the number of cubic yards needed. A cubic yard will cover approximately 80 square feet of surface to a depth of $3^{1}/2$ inches (the typical thickness of a walkway and a 2-×-4-inch form board).

To determine the quantity of concrete needed, calculate the total square footage of your walkway (length times width) and divide by 80. The answer will tell you the number of cubic yards of concrete (based on a standard depth of $3^{1}/2$ inches) needed to pour your walkway. You would need 3 cubic yards of concrete to pour a walkway $3^{1}/2$ inches deep, 4 feet wide, and 60 feet long:

$$4' \times 60' = \frac{240 \text{ ft}^2}{80 \text{ ft}^2/\text{yd}^3} = 3 \text{ yds}^3$$

If the walkway will be other than $3^{1}/2$ inches thick, you must calculate a little differently: the length × width × depth = the number of cubic feet of area in your pour. Next, divide the number of cubic feet by 27 to get the number of cubic yards needed: 27 ft³ = 1 yd³. Approximately 4¹/₂ cubic yards will be needed to pour a walkway 4 feet wide, 60 feet long, and 6 inches deep (thick):

$$60' \times 4' \times 0.5' = \frac{120 \text{ ft}^3}{27 \text{ ft}^3/\text{yd}^3} = 4.44 \text{ yds}^3 \text{ or appx. } 4^1/_2 \text{ yds}^3$$

Given these figures, your supplier will be able to provide the concrete you need. It is always better to have a little extra than not enough, so your supplier might suggest that you add a cushion of 5 percent over your estimate. When your truckload of concrete arrives, make sure you have plenty of strong, willing people on hand. Sometimes, a truck cannot pour directly into your forms. In this case, arrange for assistants and wheelbarrows to haul the concrete to where it is needed.

Pouring

Concrete is best poured in the early morning and, if possible, on dry days that are above freezing. Having help and your tools ready before the pour is a must. You must be able to finish the surface quicker than it dries to avoid problems.

Concrete should have only enough water to allow it to flow, not to create a watery, thin mixture. Pour the concrete as near its final location as possible. It is best to avoid pulling or dragging the concrete excessively. Concrete can be worked into corners and against forms with a square-edged shovel (flat shovel). Be careful against the forms. You do not want to bow the forms.

Concrete has a percentage of course aggregates that must be worked below the surface but not driven to the bottom of the pour. Once the forms are filled, the area is screeded. This is accomplished by moving a 2×4 (the screed) back and forth against the forms. Any excess concrete is moved ahead of the screed or used to fill in any low areas behind the screed area. This screed work must be done as quickly as possible after pouring. If "bleed water" collects on the surface before screeding, a possibility exists that the surface will dust or scale.

Finishing

Finishing is one of the most critical steps for producing a successful walkway surface. After the concrete has been screeded, it is time to finish. The concrete should be able to sustain foot pressure without damage and the surface should be free of water sheen. A bull float, a long-handled float with a wide blade, is first used to smooth out the surface. A darby, best used for narrow areas such as walkways, is similar to a bull float except that it does not have a long handle.

Brick walkways

Brick is considered by many to be the most ideal paving material in gardens. Brick comes in a multitude of colors and sizes and is both nonglare and skid-proof. It can also be installed in an endless variety of patterns and combinations (FIG. 5-6). The attraction for the professional and the do-it-yourselfer is great. It is best to avoid complex patterns because of the extra work of cutting and installing individual bricks. The simplicity or complexity, however, depends on personal choice and ability.

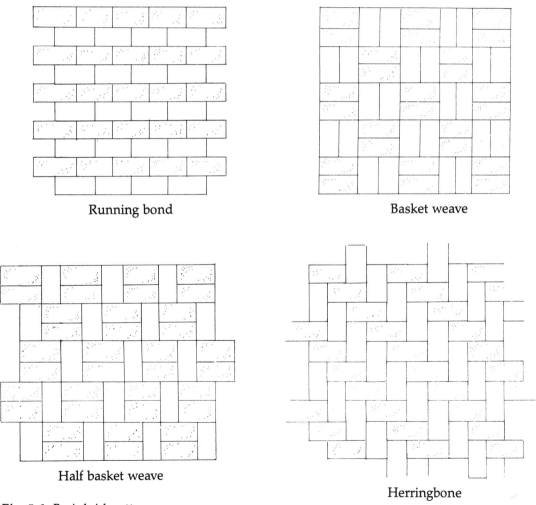

Running bond

Basket weave

Half basket weave

Herringbone

Fig. 5-6. Basic brick patterns.

It is important to accurately estimate the number of bricks your project will require. Bricks, like many products with color, are manufactured in groups. To ensure that your colors match, you must order bricks from the same group. Ordering additional bricks at a later date might yield a slightly different color or tint. In severe winter conditions, it is advisable to order a weatherproof brick. Check with your local brick supplier for this special brick.

A common brick is approximately $3^3/4$ inches wide $\times 2^1/4$ inches thick $\times 8$ inches long and will weigh a couple of pounds. Because of this weight, it is usually better to have bricks delivered to your home rather than make multiple trips in a car or small pickup truck. A standard unit of bricks is a pallet containing 500 bricks. Most suppliers would rather deliver full pallets but arrangements might be made to split a pallet. Plan to be home when the bricks are delivered and make sure they are unloaded as close to the work area as possible without having them in the way. Moving a thousand bricks placed in the wrong area can create a lot of unnecessary extra work.

After completing the five basic steps (discussed earlier in the chapter), you need to decide if the brick is to be set in a concrete or sand base.

Concrete base

Brick can be laid on a newly poured slab of concrete or on top of an existing slab. When setting brick on an existing slab, remember that the finished grade will be the thickness of the brick plus approximately a $3/4$-inch bed of new mortar. Bricks are set into mortar by lightly pushing evenly on the top surface. To encourage a better bond, bricks should be wet with a hose before setting them in mortar. Before filling the joints with mortar, the bricks should be level and spaced evenly, about $1/4$ inch.

A typical mortar mix consists of 1 part cement to $3^1/2$ parts sharp sand plus $1/2$ part lime. If color is to be added, it is usually mixed well with the other dry ingredients. Enough water is added to the dry mix so that it becomes a buttery consistency.

Premixed and packaged mortar might be available in your area. This is a convenient method for small areas but it is usually too cost-prohibitive for large projects. When placing mortar into joints, use a grout bag to help avoid excess mortar on the bricks. Clean the brick surface of excess mortar before it cures to avoid massive labor to clean later. When the mortar cures completely, you'll be able to proudly walk through your garden on your new walkway.

Sand base

To keep bricks from shifting or tilting, you'll need a 1-inch base of sand that is firmly packed. If you have severe winters or are subject to frost heaving, the base should be 4 inches deep and extend 4 inches wider than the walkway width. This extra base minimizes heaving.

The proper depth of the finished base (in relation to the finished grade), is achieved with the use of a screed. A straight 2×4 is notched for the brick thickness. The screed board is then set on the edge board and drawn across the sand base. Excess sand is pushed ahead of the screed while low spots are filled and firmly packed. A slightly high bed (approximately 1/4 inch) will allow for setting the bricks. The brick is laid on the sand base and set with a rubber mallet. A short length of 2×4 laid over the brick and tapped with a claw hammer is a workable alternative. Bricks set in either of these two ways will minimize breakage.

Joints can be tightly set or spaced for filling with dry mortar or wet mortar mix from a grout bag. Fine sand is usually swept into tight joints to complete the installation. On open-space joints, wet mix mortar applied with a grout bag will hold the bricks a little more firmly. Dry mix mortar swept into the joints can be carefully wet with a hose to set up the curing process. Joints filled with mortar (wet or dry) can be smoothed (called *pointing*) using a joint tool or a short length of 3/4-inch pipe.

If your walkway meanders through a garden, a more natural look can be achieved if joints are filled with soil. This way, grass or ground covers can be grown between the bricks.

No matter how carefully you chose a pattern to avoid cutting bricks, cutting cannot be completely avoided. Bricks are generally classed as soft bricks or hardened bricks. A soft brick will cut easily using a brick set (chisel) hit sharply with a hammer. Place a brick on a firm surface and score along the cutting line with a wide chisel, or *brick set*. Hold the brick set upright with the bevel facing away from you. Hit firmly with a 5-pound, hand-held sledgehammer. To finish cutting, angle the brick set towards you slightly and hit again. Hard bricks, however, must be cut using masonry blades. Your circular saw can be fitted with a masonry blade. Construct a jig by nailing two pieces of a 2×4 to a piece of plywood. Space them so that a brick can rest between them. Set your saw to make a shallow, 1/4-inch cut and score the brick along the cutting line. Turn the brick over and score the backside. Using a mason's hammer, tap the unwanted piece of brick to free the desired portion along the cut line. Always wear gloves and goggles for safety. When a large number of bricks are to be cut accurately, a circular saw and abrasive blade are the tools to use. A better choice is to check with a local tool rental company. Saws made specifically for brick cutting make your job easier and more enjoyable.

Because bricks set on sand are not as permanent as when set in concrete, there must be a retainer against both edges of the walkway. Bricks set on edge or on end, as well as decay-resistant wood, act as excellent "curbs" to hold the walkway in place.

Other materials

Natural stone, slate, and flagstone work well for beautiful and service-able walkways. If locally available, the cost can be reasonable. Because of the high cost of shipping heavy materials, however, it is usually cost-prohibitive the farther you are from the source.

Flagstone is handled much the same way as brick, cutting soft stone with a brick set and hard stone with a masonry blade. Stones can be set in concrete or sand. If sand is used for the base, it must be increased to 2 inches in mild climates and 6 inches in severe winter climates. Stones are not set in place through tapping but rather shifted and settled into place. Joints are handled in the same manner as brick.

Precast concrete pavers

The variety of precast concrete pavers is wide, offering varying sizes from 12 to 30 inches standard and shapes such as circles, squares, rectangles, and hexagons. Color and surface finishes are also available in a wide range of choices.

Installing concrete pavers is similar to installing brick. One point you must remember is that pavers can have varying thicknesses depending on the style. In this case, just adjust the base with the finished grade to allow for the thickness of the style you have chosen.

Interlocking paving blocks

Interlocking paving blocks, a precast paver (bricklike unit), are relatively new. The geometric shape of each unit is cast so that multiple units link together or interlock to form a very tight, stable surface. The basic principles of brick installation apply to interlocking pavers. Check with your local supplier for additional tips on how to best install this unique surfacing material.

Informal pavings

It is sometimes necessary or desirable to surface a garden with a material that is softer in appearance than brick or concrete. The alternative is to use a surface material that will drain well, handle foot traffic comfortably, and look good (FIGS. 5-7 through 5-11). To minimize weeds, a weed barrier cloth can be purchased and installed beneath the surface material. This weed barrier cloth allows water to penetrate but retards weed growth. Tar paper and plastic have been used in the past but are inferior choices. Both tend to adversely affect drainage and are unsightly if displaced. Grade your walkway area to provide proper drainage, then simply wheelbarrow your choice in place and rake level.

Some of the materials you might consider are brick dust, crushed gravel, round stone, and bark mulch. Check local suppliers for other possible choices. Most of these casual or informal surface materials will need to be edged to avoid a scattered, unkempt look.

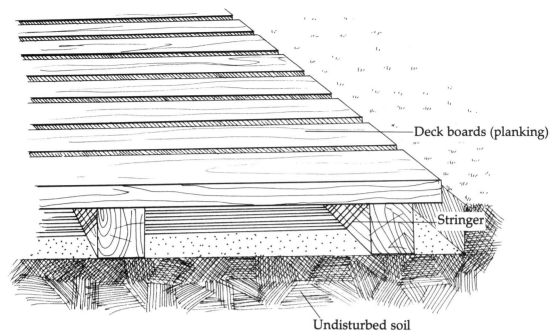

Deck boards (planking)

Stringer

Undisturbed soil

Fig. 5-7. Wood planking used as a boardwalk.

Fig. 5-8. This boardwalk serves the function of tying two areas together.

Fig. 5-9. Boardwalks can assume a variety of shapes to fit your environment.

Fig. 5-10. Wood rounds.

When a large number of bricks are to be cut accurately, a circular saw and abrasive blade are the tools to use. Construct a jig by nailing two pieces of a 2×4 to a piece of plywood. Space them so that a brick can rest between them. Set your saw to make a shallow, 1/4-inch cut and score the brick along the cutting line. Turn the brick over and score the backside. Using a mason's hammer, tap the unwanted piece of brick to free the desired portion along the cut line. Always wear gloves and goggles for safety.

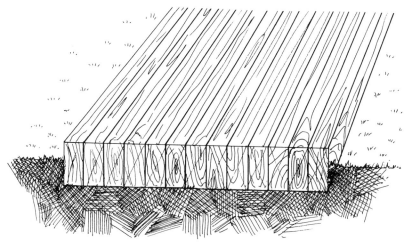

Fig. 5-11. Timbers laid on edge and embedded in the soil provide a unique walkway.

Constructing steps

If a main entry is to have steps, they must have adequate space for several people to arrive at the same time. They must also be safe and inviting. The materials you choose should harmonize with adjacent structures and paving. For this reason, materials such as brick, stone, wood, and concrete can be used.

It is important to work out your steps on graph paper before beginning any construction. Remember that certain construction projects require local permits. Refer to chapter 1 for a more detailed discussion on construction permits.

You should be familiar with a few common terms and concepts before you design steps. The horizontal or flat surface of a step is called the *tread* and the vertical surface is called the *riser*. The ideal riser/tread ratio is when the depth of the tread plus twice the riser height equals between 25 and 27 inches. The best combination for ease and safety in walking is a 6-inch riser with a 15-inch tread. Dimensions might vary, but the tread to riser ratio remains constant. Risers should be no less than 4 inches nor higher than 7 inches. Treads should never be shallower than 11 inches. In any single flight of steps, the dimensions of the risers and treads should be uniform.

When designing steps, you need to measure the slope. To measure the slope, you'll need to set up a simple device to determine the rise and run (see FIG. 5-12). The distance A-B measures the rise and A-C is the minimum horizontal distance your steps will cover, called the *run*. To calculate the number of steps and dimensions needed for a particular run, divide the rise of the slope by the desired riser height of the steps. Next, multiply your tread size, using the tread/riser formula, by the number of steps. The result should approximately equal the run from A to C. Make adjustments to fit the slope. There are many different varieties that can be used to achieve the desired effect. See FIGS. 5-13 through 5-18.

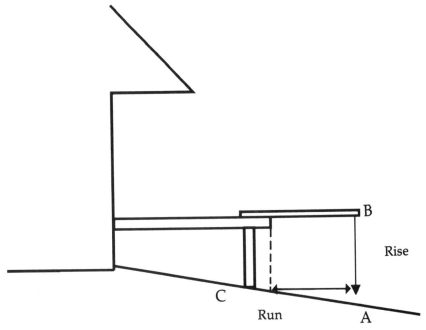

Fig. 5-12. A plumb bob suspended on a 2×4 at deck height determines rise and run (span) of stairway.

Fig. 5-13. Plantings can help soften steps and invite the passerby.

Fig. 5-14. Broad steps can emphasize a front entry.

Fig. 5-15. Brick-faced concrete steps.

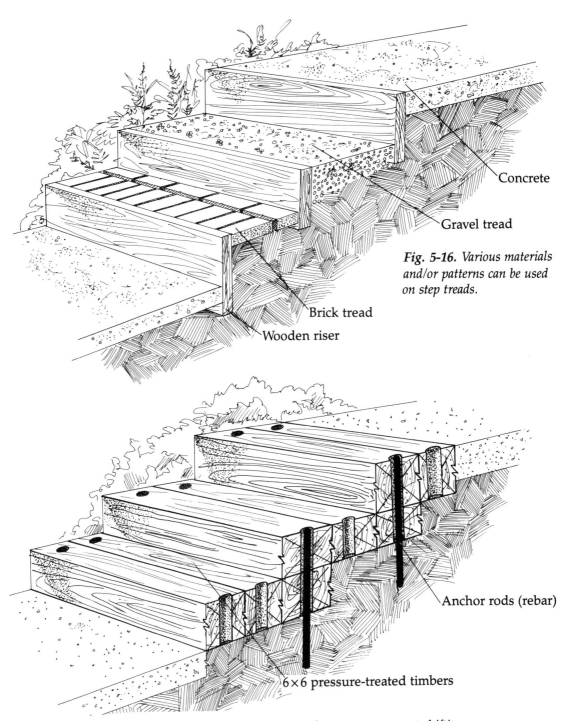

Concrete

Gravel tread

Fig. 5-16. Various materials and/or patterns can be used on step treads.

Brick tread

Wooden riser

Anchor rods (rebar)

6×6 pressure-treated timbers

Fig. 5-17. Rebar must be used on these 6×6 timbers used as steps to prevent shifting.

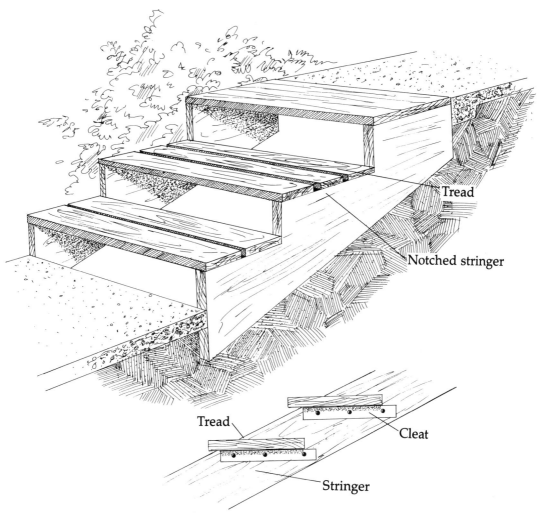

Fig. 5-18. Wooden treads can be attached on cleats or a notched stringer.

6

Walls

Few man-made structures have as much impact on the landscape as walls and fences. Walls and fences define the character and function of a landscape. From the simple stone walls in farm fields (defining boundaries and ridding the land of obstructions to the plow) to elaborate wrought iron fences used purely for aesthetics in the garden. Many other examples might include picket fences for privacy, brick or wood fences to divide gardens, and seawalls or breakwaters to protect.

Walls and fences have slightly different historical functions. Walls form a boundary to protect property from trespassers, create shelter from wind and rain, provide privacy, and retain soil and changes in grade. Fences were originally intended to divide and protect properties but were not expected to shelter or provide privacy. The idea was that fences don't hide views and provide privacy, but rather help to accentuate views.

A wall should be designed so that it can be enjoyed year-round. During the growing season, it can show off potted plants, flower beds, trees, and shrubs. In other seasons, a wall can add form to a winter landscape covered with snow or act as a background for unique deciduous trees and shrubs.

Walls can be finished smooth or textured, built as a solid unit or baffled, and can be almost any color.

Walls can provide the skeleton of your garden upon which other elements depend for support. Walls tie in well with other permanent features, such as steps, garden pools, gazebos, and trellises. Walls need not always be built in straight lines either. Sweeping curves, semicircles, arcs, and angles can add interest to your wall, garden, and landscape.

Today, whether you build a wall or a fence, it must fit your lifestyle, provide screening, and enhance privacy in certain areas and visual enhancement in others. Fences should be aesthetically pleasing, add to the total picture, and not be at odds with the environment.

Brick and block walls

For most do-it-yourselfers, low, straight walls constructed of block or brick are the easiest to build. Brick and block are easy to use because of their uniform size, with bricks even easier to set because of their relative light weight.

As with any construction project, several things must be done before work begins. If the wall is to be located anywhere near your property line, the property line's location must be accurately determined. Some properties have permanent markers that locate all corners of a yard. In this case, you need only connect the corners with a straight line to outline the property boundary.

When building anything permanent, it is best not to guess. If you are wrong, it can cause a lot of frustration and extra expense to correct the mistake. Prior to construction, hire a surveyor to resurvey your property and set permanent markers. Check the yellow pages or a real estate office for the name of a local surveying firm.

You will also need to contact the local building inspector's office. Most communities have a set of guidelines that regulate building projects, and walls are no exception. These ordinances can limit the overall size, height, material, character, or appearance of your wall. They also set the standards for setbacks. Setbacks are the required distances that permanent buildings and other structures must be set back from property lines.

Another important aspect of the building inspector's review of your project is its overall safety. The inspector will check to see that strength and stability are incorporated into your construction so that it does not become a public hazard.

Low walls, up to a foot high, and free-standing units, need not be more than 4 inches thick. Retaining walls and walls 1 foot high or greater should be approximately 8 inches thick. If the wall is to be used as a seat wall (16 to 18 inches high), a thickness of 12 inches is recommended.

All walls should be set on a proper foundation. A general rule of thumb suggests that the footing be as thick as the width of the wall. Footings must be below the frostline, particularly in areas that experience heavy frost activity. The width of the footing should be double the thickness of the wall. An 8-inch-thick wall would be located in the center of a 16-inch-wide footing that is 8 inches deep.

If the wall is to be used as a seat, bolts should be embedded in the mortar or concrete so that planks can be secured to the top of the masonry wall. Any wood can be used, but the seat will last longer if it is made of either decay-resistant wood (redwood, cedar, or pressure-treated) or a regular schedule of preserving is implemented. To be comfortable and safe from splinters, the wood should be knot-free, clear wood that has been well sanded and sealed.

Stone walls

Stone walls can be very beautiful. While stone can be considerably more expensive and more difficult to handle, a well-built stone wall is usually worth the extra effort. Stone walls can be constructed using mortar or dry laid.

If mortar is used, it should be a rich mixture, having increased cement content for a stronger joint. A mixture of $1^1/_2$ parts cement ($^1/_2$ part more than usual), 1 part lime, and 3 parts clean, fine sand with sufficient water to achieve the consistency of soft mud, will yield an ideal mortar for stone walls.

Set the first course of stones in mortar level on the footing. The wall needs to be built with a batter, or a backward slope from the base of the wall to the cap. A ratio of 2 inches to every 2 feet of wall height should be observed for a mortared stone wall. Continue setting each course in mortar, observing the proper batter until the finished cap height is reached.

When laying stone, it is important to check the grain of each piece of stone. The grain, or lengthwise streaks in the stone, should be laid so that they are parallel to the ground. It is very rare that the grain of a stone be vertical in nature. Placing stones vertical destroys the natural look of the wall and the final effect might resemble a pile of rocks dumped into place rather then set in harmony with your landscape.

Dry-laid walls need not be built on a footing, but will require a steeper batter. A ratio of 3 to 4 inches per 2 feet of wall height is best. Dig a trench approximately 6 to 18 inches deep and backfill with crushed stone that is compacted well by tamping. Set the base stones on this crushed stone. Their own weight and gravity will hold the stones in the wall in place. Well-built stone wall pieces fit together completely, almost as if they were pieces of a jigsaw puzzle.

All walls benefit from a cap because it prevents them from deteriorating due to weathering. Caps add the finishing touch. Contrasting bricks and ornamental concrete blocks, coping blocks, tiles, and wood all work well as caps.

Any naturally occurring, or planned for, cavities, can be filled with topsoil and planted with a variety of plants that will enhance the wall's beauty. Figure 6-1 lists some such plants.

Botanical Name	Common Name	Plant Type
Ajuga reptans	Bugle-weed	Ground cover
Arabis alplna	Rockcress	Herb
Arctostaphylos uva-ursi	Bearberry	Ground cover
Calluna vulgaris	Heather	Perennial evergreen
Chionodoxa lucillae	Glory-of-the-snow	Bulb
Dicentra eximia	Wild bleeding-heart	Perennial
Eranthis hyemalis	Winter-aconite	Bulb
Erica camea	Heath	Perennial evergreen
Euonymus fortunei minimus	Dwarf winter-creeper	Ground cover
Iberis sempervirens	Candytuft	Annual
Narcissus species	Daffodils	Bulb
Phlox subulata	Moss-pink	Perennial
Primula polyantha	Primrose	Perennial
Sedum album	White stonecrop	Perennial
Sedum spurium	Stonecrop	Perennial
Sempervivum soboliferum	Hen and chickens	Perennial
Thymus serpyllum	Thyme	Herb

Fig. 6-1. Easy culture plants, adaptable to rock gardens and planting pockets found in rock walls.

Poured concrete walls

Low walls constructed of concrete are limited by the ability to build a retaining form. Because concrete is a fluid material, however, it can be placed to conform to any construction work in your yard with a little ingenuity.

Lumber 1 inch thick or greater can be used to build forms. Make sure that forms are well braced. Secure 2×4s to the form every 4 to 5 feet on straight sections, closer on curves, and use plenty of supporting stakes.

Because concrete is fluid, it will conform to the texture of wooden forms. For a smooth face, use exterior grade plywood for the forms. To highlight the grain, sandblast the wood. The grain will then be transferred to the finished wall surface. Concrete walls can also be painted, stuccoed, or plastered.

When placing concrete, it is important that the concrete be spread along the length of the wall, building up layers of 6- to 8-inch thicknesses. Remove any air pockets by tamping the newly placed concrete with a 2×4.

To allow for proper setting up, or curing, of the wall, forms should remain in place for at least one week. To prevent the concrete from drying too fast, cover it with a canvas, burlap, or plastic sheet. Remove the cover daily and sprinkle the wall with a water hose. Replace the covering after dampening the wall.

A poured concrete wall of 2 feet in height should be capped with a seat. All walls benefit from a cap because it prevents them from deteriorating due to weathering. Caps also add the finishing touch to a poured wall. Bricks, ornamental concrete blocks, coping blocks, tiles, and wood all work well as caps.

After the concrete has cured, a mortar mix is used to secure all but wood materials as a cap. If wood for a seat is to be installed, the anchor bolts should be set into the wet concrete before it has cured too much. Because most walls are built with a stiff concrete mix, the bolts can be set in place after the concrete is placed in the forms. Check to make sure they do not sink into the wall, however.

Retaining walls

Retaining walls are designed to retain the slope of a hillside when the pitch of the slope is changed or to retain the soil around the roots of a tree that is to be saved. If an area of your property is "hilly" and you want to level or flatten a section, you might need to build a wall that is not only aesthetic, but structurally strong.

If you need a wall that stands higher than 3 feet, it is advisable to consult a professional. A wall can have several tons of pressure exerted upon it by uphill soil. For this reason, not only is it best to have tall walls engineered and designed by a professional, but many communities require the use of a licensed engineer. Short walls, however, can be designed by the do-it-yourselfer who remembers a few rules:

- No slope is totally static or stable. Given enough rain and/or in some areas, seismic activity, all slopes move materials from the top to the bottom.
- The base of your wall should be set on undisturbed soil, not filled soil.
- The amount of excavation should be kept to a minimum. Select a site at the bottom of a gentle slope and fill behind the wall.
- All walls must be anchored securely so that neither the wall nor the slope shifts.

Walls built on a hillside are more pleasing and easier to install if sections of the wall are stepped down from level to level. The stepped sections allow for the creation of terraces when placed several feet apart.

All retaining walls must be designed to allow for adequate drainage. If water is allowed to build up without a means of dispersal, the wall might collapse. Several methods of drainage are available.

At the surface, a shallow ditch can be made to collect and divert water. A backfill of gravel at the wall's base will facilitate the collection of subsurface water. Disposing of the subsurface water could be done with a 4- to 6-inch perforated drainpipe that channels the water away from the wall.

An alternate method would be to place evenly spaced weep holes at the wall's base. These ground-level holes might need a gutterlike depression to collect and channel rainwater to prevent it from running onto your patio or lawn. When installing pipes and/or weep holes, make sure they are pitched, or sloped, to allow the constant, positive flow of water to disposal areas.

As mentioned earlier, retaining walls and walls 1 foot high or greater should be approximately 8 inches thick. If the wall is to be used as a seat wall (16 to 18 inches high), a thickness of 12 inches is recommended.

Poured concrete walls

Poured concrete walls used as retaining walls must be treated a little differently than free-standing walls. When a wall retains a grade change, it will also retain moisture in the soil behind the wall. This moisture, if allowed to collect, can cause a great deal of pressure on the wall. If this pressure is not relieved, the wall can collapse. Relief is provided through weep holes. Pipes flush with the outside of the wall and extending back into the retained soil, placed every 4 to 6 feet, allow adequate drainage for very low walls or where the accumulation of moisture is expected to be at a minimum.

If the amount of moisture to collect and disperse is great because of heavy rainfalls, then drain tiles might be needed to carry the water away from the wall. Backfilling the wall with coarse aggregates set over drain tiles will direct the collection and disposal of water to the far end of the wall. If weep holes are used, a gutter can be installed at the foot of the wall to channel water away from walks and patios.

7

Planter boxes

Raised planter beds can be used in any yard to enhance the landscape. On very flat terrain, a raised bed provides much-needed visual relief. On a sloping property, a raised bed can be used with low retaining walls to provide level areas for planting. Raised beds can enhance patios by providing vertical relief or to separate areas. In areas that are plagued by ground rodents, a raised planter box could deter pests. Planters can be used for growing vegetables, herbs, cut flowers, or special plants. If built at an appropriate height, a cap can be installed to provide a seat. Raised beds can be used for a multitude of other landscape settings as well:

- Enhance a patio's pattern.
- Designate parking space and direct foot traffic in parking areas.
- Retain a section of hill on steep grade changes when built as a series of terraces.
- Provide a multilevel garden area on flat ground by stacking the raised beds.

Gardening beds

Elevated planter boxes make gardening more pleasurable for the novice and pro alike. The convenient height makes gardening easier and is especially useful for those gardeners who have physical difficulty working at ground level. Because a raised bed will warm more quickly than a regular garden bed, it can be worked earlier in the spring. A planter box allows the gardener to modify harsh soil conditions by backfilling with a soil that satisfies special planting requirements, such as sand for a desert garden or compost-rich for vegetable gardening.

Construction

Most raised beds are simple to construct. The size and shape are limited only by your gardening needs and imagination. Beds can be constructed of brick, concrete, railroad ties, or pressure-treated lumber. The most important construction element of any raised bed is adequate drainage. If the box is constructed above open soil, drainage might be automatic. If the raised bed is for a patio or other impervious material, artificial drainage must be provided. Loose gravel and weep holes in the bottom of a planter usually provide proper drainage.

For ease of care, a raised bed should be no wider than 3 feet, if access is provided only from one side. Free-standing beds with access from both sides can be as wide as 6 feet without the need to walk into the bed.

Tree boxes

If you are building a planter box to go around a shade tree and must change the grade, it is important to try and retain the original grade over the root zone. Just a few inches of fill on top of the root zone will deprive the tree roots of essential oxygen. If space permits, the box should be as large as the tree's drip line. If the grade needs to be lowered, the retaining box will hold the original soil at the base of the tree. The box can be constructed of dimensional lumber or railroad ties.

To retain soil away from a tree when the grade needs to be raised, a well or pit must be built. For this type of box, build the wall around the base of the tree then add fill to the outside. If you cannot, or do not want, an open pit, the well can be filled with large decorative stones. The stones are added to the pit as a final step and will permit air and water to penetrate to the root zone.

When building a raised bed that adjoins a building, it is necessary to prevent moisture from the bed from seeping into the building. A backing layer of waterproof material works well with wood construction. If the box is not built with a back, the building surface will need to have some type of waterproofing treatment. A local lumberyard or building supply dealer should be able to suggest the best material for your area.

Raised beds and flower pots are not the only places to plant color for your garden. Wooden boxes have the advantage of being built to your specific design needs. They can be taller, longer, and wider than pots. Boxes can be set on patios, decks, balconies, railings, or below windows (FIGS. 7-1 and 7-2).

Fig. 7-1. *A planter box along a walkway defines the area and directs traffic.*

Fig. 7-2. *Multilevel planter boxes tie in with this house's architecture.*

Finishing touches

To add interest to your boxes or planters, they can be set off by placing them on a pedestal or stand. Stumps, sections of railroad ties, telephone poles, or driftwood all work well as unique and aesthetically pleasing stands.

Once the basic box is made, it can be modified with the simple addition of a trellis. A single panel of 1×3s can be built and attached at an angle and used for growing melons. As the watermelons or cantaloupes develop on the vine, a shelf can be added to the trellis beneath the fruit. These portable shelves provide support wherever needed.

Attach a trellis to two boxes and create an A-frame unit. Growing cucumbers or tomatoes in this type of structure provides an adventure for children. They will be able to walk under this tunnel of fruit at the right height for them to harvest.

8

Water features

Few things so easily set a mood in a garden as water. The faint sound of water trickling down a waterfall or the gentle cascading of a fountain draws the passerby into a relaxing and exotic environment. A water feature might be that unique "something extra" your garden needs. A water garden is a mini-ecosystem created by growing and nurturing aquatic plants and fish.

Water gardens can be enjoyed by urban and rural dwellers alike. Size need not be a factor when considering a water feature. There are many types of water features that will blend with practically any garden. A birdbath is helpful for attracting birds, while a pond might serve as a spectacular display of aquatic plants or fish. Water gardens are one of the most popular do-it-yourself projects that not only boosts property value, but enhances your garden as well.

The cultivation of lotus plants, papyrus, and water lilies dates back to the ancient Egyptians. Water gardens have also been a popular element of European gardens for centuries. Classic statuary, introduced by Greeks and Romans, added extravagant flair to water gardens, as can be seen in the formal ponds and fountains at the Tivoli Gardens in Rome and Versailles in France. Not to be forgotten, is the artistic representation and time-honored tradition of oriental landscapes incorporating exotic water gardens. As you will see in this chapter, water features need not be large or elaborate to create a mood.

Pools for aquatic plants and fish are an easy do-it-yourself project. A wide variety of pond kits are available on the market. The kits might include a vinyl pond liner or a preformed shell. Both produce attractive, finished projects. The choice of kit will depend on your locality and personal preference. If you choose not to purchase a kit, it is still possible to have a reflecting pond by constructing it on site.

Garden ponds built on site follow no set patterns. They can, and should, conform to your own unique garden. They can be long and narrow, round, oval, or irregular in shape. For extra effect, they can be constructed with walls high enough to be capped for sitting.

Water gardens can even be built with portability in mind. Submersible pumps make it unnecessary to have permanent plumbing hookups. The pumps can recirculate water through a gravel base that acts as a large filter. If the pond is permanent, the plumbing required is very simple. An inlet for water should be provided as well as a gravity drain at the bottom of the pond. An overflow to maintain a constant water level can be tied into the drain system.

Water circulation is provided by submersible pumps. These pumps can be simple, providing only circulation of the water, or showy, with different types of fountain heads. The Little Giant Pump Company has a wide range of pumps that can power an interesting array of fountain heads.

Design considerations

Water gardens, if carefully planned, can be installed by one or two people in a weekend. In order that your garden might be enjoyed from inside your house as well as from outside, locate it so that it can be seen from a strategic window or patio door. Other factors equally important to consider are:

- Exposure to sunlight. Water gardens perform best with five to ten hours of direct sunlight a day. In the southern United States, water gardens benefit from mid to late afternoon shade.

- Drainage. To prevent problems to your liner, soil should be well drained. Wet soil can distort a pond liner while sandy soil needs special preparation to prevent caving in.

- Nearness to trees. Water gardens located near trees can encounter problems with roots growing into the liner. Another problem caused by trees is the accumulation of leaves in the water. Decaying leaves can create toxic conditions for fish and plant life as well as clogging pumps and filters.

- Availability of electricity and water. Due to evaporation, most ponds will need to be topped off with additional water. If a permanent source of water is not provided, then a convenient hose should be available. Most ponds have recirculating pumps, water-falls, or lighting that will require electricity. Check local codes to determine electrical restrictions near water. Most communities will require the hiring of a licensed electrical contractor.

- Space allocation. The size of the yard as well as any existing or planned landscaping and landscape features will determine how large or small your water garden should be.
- Depth. Shallow ponds tend to encourage excessive algae growth. A pond 18 to 24 inches deep will provide a better environment for plants and fish with reduced algae accumulation. In colder climates, it is better to favor deeper ponds so that fish can overwinter in the pond without dying. Check your local zoning ordinances for the codes governing the installation of deep ponds. Many codes will require fencing to enclose the pond area.

A garden pond can be created using one of three methods of installation: flexible plastic liners, prefabricated fiberglass ponds (usually a kit), or a concrete-lined pond. Flexible plastic liners are inexpensive and can be cut to almost any shape. Prefabricated fiberglass ponds are generally more durable but are also usually more expensive. The most permanent installation is a concrete-lined pond.

Installing a concrete pool

A simple way to visualize a pond is to think of a bowl of water. The bowl has sides that restrict the outside boundaries of the reflecting pond area. In the garden, the edges of the area are bound by many materials, such as brick, wood, or concrete. No matter what material you choose, it must be able to hold water without leaking. You are, essentially, building a box that is watertight and submerging it into the ground.

Concrete is a very common pond material and is easy to work into irregular shapes with contoured bottoms. Unless the pond is very large, it is best to mix the concrete on site. A power mixer can be an inexpensive timesaver for this process. The concrete used should be a dry mix, not runny and pourable. A shovelful of concrete should remain in a blob when dropped on the ground. A good mixture is 1 part cement to 2 parts sand, 3 parts gravel, and only a very little water.

Remove the soil from the proposed pond area and smooth out the contours of the bottom. Because concrete is to be the wall, extra care is not needed as with liner installation. Cut reinforcing wire into pieces that can be worked into the contour of your pond. Several pieces might be needed and overlapped. Support the wire away from all sides and the bottom so that it will be completely surrounded by concrete.

With wire in place, concrete can be set into the pond. Place the stiff mix into the bottom and then work your way up the side walls. Make sure that the concrete gets into and around all of the wire. If the pond size is not too deep, positioning a board across the top will help to place and work the concrete.

Work the concrete with a trowel, getting the surface as smooth as possible. A smooth-finished surface is much easier to keep clean. After the concrete has cured for five to seven days, it can be painted. The painted pond will give the illusion of depth. Special waterproof pond paint is available. Dark colors, such as black, green, and brown, are commonly used. Other colors might be available but ponds are usually less attractive with wild colors. Follow the label directions for application and drying times. If plants or fish are to be added, check carefully that the paint you use is nontoxic.

Installing a kit

Materials needed to install a pond kit include the liner or prefabricated pool, pick, shovel, rake, wheelbarrow, heavy rope or garden hose, level, sand, coping material, aquatic plants, and water treatment supplies. Optional materials include a submersible pump, fountain, waterfall, fish, and underwater lighting. Be sure to purchase enough liner to allow for a 6-inch overlap.

Using a heavy rope or garden hose, lay out the shape of the pond in the yard. If the shape is geometric (square, oval, circle), lay it out accordingly. If installing a prefabricated pond, make the outline 2 inches larger in all directions.

Dig a hole conforming to the shape's outline and to a depth 3 inches deeper than the pond bottom. This 3-inch layer will be backfilled with sand to provide a uniform base for the pond. Drainage can be accomplished with perforated pipes running under the pond or a hole backfilled with coarse stones. As mentioned earlier, a drain is not a necessity, but if one can be installed, it makes caring for your pond a much easier job.

A 2-foot-deep pond is adequate for most reflecting and planted ponds. If you want to add taller plants or provide a permanent home for fish, a depth of 4 feet is better. Remember to check local ordinances. Some communities might not allow a deep pond because of the potential drowning hazard. If a deeper pond is allowed, the regulations might require adequate protection to minimize the possibility of someone falling into the pond.

Pools are best constructed with shelves that can provide different planting depths. A shelf can be 9 to 12 inches wide around the entire perimeter or only in certain areas. These shelves can provide a habitat for boggy plants such as cattails. When digging the hole, be careful to remove all rocks, roots, and any other debris that could create a problem for the liner.

Backfill the excavation with approximately 3 inches of damp sand to provide a base for the liner. Approximately 1 ton of sand will cover an area of 40 square feet.

Center the liner over the excavation and push it into the corners. In corners and around curves, the liner can be folded into pleats (never cut). Slowly start filling the pond with water, smoothing out folds and wrinkles.

When the pond is completely filled, any surplus liner can be trimmed from the edges. There should be about 6 inches of overlap that will be covered with a coping material. Typical coping materials include field stone, bricks, and tiles.

If your design includes a fountain, waterfall, or recirculating pump, now is the time to install it. Follow the manufacturer's instructions.

Before stocking the pond, chlorine levels must be neutralized. Check with your local water-garden supplier for procedures to counteract chlorine.

Fountains and waterfalls

Fountains give shape to water gardens. In addition to providing a focal point, the trickling water is pleasing to the eyes and ears (FIG. 8-1). When installing either a fountain or waterfall, however, it is important to remember that neither feature should dwarf or be dwarfed by the pond.

Fig. 8-1. A simple pool appears more elegant with a simple fountain.

Fountains and waterfalls filter and recirculate water, an important feature for the health of your pond. Many garden supply centers or mail-order firms offer a wide range of fountain styles, from the very simple jet nozzle to elaborate patterns produced with ornate statuary.

Waterfalls can be purchased prefabricated or constructed by building a slope of soil and then covering it with the same liner material used in the pond. Plastic tubing connected to a pump at the base of the waterfall provides water to the head of the waterfall. Figure 8-2 illustrates the mechanics of a simple fountain.

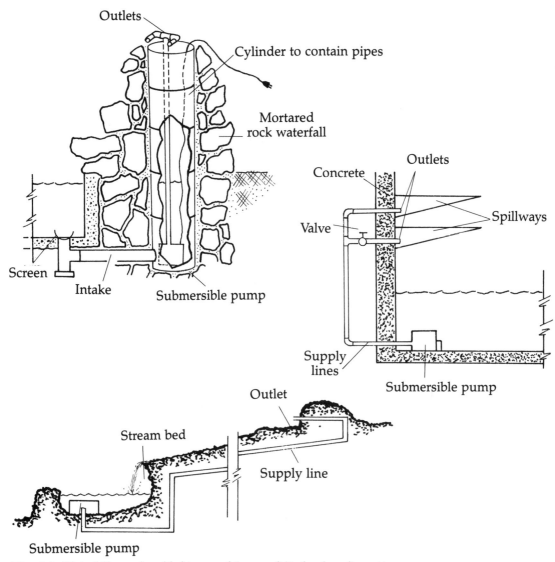

Fig. 8-2. Waterfalls can be added to a pool in a multitude of configurations.

Stocking Plants

Water gardens offer a unique environment for a culture of plants not able to grow elsewhere. The water garden, its plants, fish, and the environment all work together as a mini-ecosystem. Plants act as an ecological balance by providing oxygen and shading. Too much sunlight in a water garden encourages algae growth. Typically, four types of plants are used to stock a pond: deep-water plants, bog plants or marginals, oxygenators, and floating plants.

When planting, it is advisable to use lined baskets, plastic tubs, or clay pots to minimize spreading and overcrowding conditions. Place plants in containers and fill with heavy garden soil. Spread a layer of pea gravel over the top of the soil to help keep it from floating in the water. Avoid using potting soil or garden soil that contains chemicals or fertilizers because it might be harmful to other aquatic life.

Once plants are potted, they can be placed in the appropriate area of the pond, as dictated by plant type. If you plan on stocking the pond with fish, wait a period of four to five weeks to allow planting to establish before introducing fish.

Deep-water plants

One of the most well known and popular aquatic deep-water group of plants is the water lily. They are colorful, highly fragrant, and easy to care for. The plants sit submerged 12 to 24 inches below the water surface with the blooms floating on the surface.

Tropical water lilies are larger, more fragrant, more colorful, and bloom more often than hearty lilies. In fact, they might bloom every day for the entire blooming season. Some varieties bloom either during the day or at night. Unfortunately, they are more susceptible to killing frosts. In areas where frost occurs, you'll need to store the plants in a protected environment such as a greenhouse. If you want to enjoy them and have no way to protect them, enjoy them as you would any annual.

Hardy lilies might have longer blooming seasons in northern regions but will have intermittent periods of dormancy (repeated weekly cycles of rest and bloom). Some hardy water lilies can survive in water depths up to 10 feet. They can survive in cold regions and, as long as the water does not freeze all the way to the root stock, they can remain in your pond all winter long. Both hearty and tropical water lilies need at least five and sometimes up to 12 hours of sunlight plus regular fertilization.

Another deep water plant related to the water lily, is the lotus. Although this plant has a shorter blooming season, spectacular leaves and seed pods (used in flower arrangements) are popular features. Lotus require at least 5 hours of sunlight and a water depth of 2 to 3 feet—plus large containers, making this plant best suited to larger ponds.

Bog plants or marginals

Boggy, shallow areas that border the margins of a pond are the environment best suited to plants such as: cattails, iris, bamboo, and papyrus. Bog plants typically grow in mud or water up to 6 inches deep. Your pond should have a shallow shelf constructed into it for the placement of these plants. A shallow, shady end of the pond is a great location for cattails because they will survive equally well in shade or full sun.

Submerged plants or oxygenators

A plant economically essential for pond health is one that is never seen above the surface. These plants slow the growth of algae, absorb excess nutrients that might cloud the water, and provide food for your fish. Hardy, inexpensive varieties such as elodea/anacharis and cabomba can be purchased from a garden pond supply store. If your pond is too small to accommodate these plants, a pump can provide aeration and oxygenation.

Floating plants

Floating plants are the easiest to grow. They need no soil; they just float on the surface of the water. Be careful, however. They can be aggressive growers that take over your pond quickly. Floating heart, water hyacinth, and floating water ferns are common floating plants.

Stocking fish

Pond fish are not only fascinating to watch but are also easy to care for. Fish serve many functions. They eat algae, mosquito larvae, and insects, as well as trim excessive plant foliage.

Aquarium or tropical fish generally are not suited for pond life. Goldfish, however, are very hearty, and can survive many years in properly designed and installed ponds. Being a member of the carp family, goldfish can grow to remarkable sizes, depending on the size of the pond it lives in. Probably the most known and popular pond fish is the Japanese Koi. These fish can grow to 2 or 3 feet in length and exhibit varied and dramatic coloring patterns. A good rule of thumb in stocking your pond is that for every square foot of water, no more than 1 to 2 inches of fish should be provided.

Fish must be acclimated to the water in the pond before they are released into the water. Floating the fish in a plastic bag on the surface for 15 to 20 minutes will help them adjust.

A pond well stocked with plant material will usually provide adequate nutrition for your fish. If you wish to provide supplemental feeding, remember to do so in moderation because excess food will not decay, causing your pond to become cloudy.

Maintenance

The survival and well-being of a water garden depends on proper and regular maintenance. The process begins immediately after installation with the control of excessive algae growth. Fish can help to minimize algae growth as well as filtering the system. Clean filters regularly so that they perform at peak. If algae growth gets out of control, an algicide can be used. Algicides are chemicals specially formulated to kill algae. Be careful using any chemical. Always read the label and follow directions completely and carefully. Be especially certain that the algicide used will not harm your fish or aquatic plant life.

The water level in the water garden needs to be regularly monitored. A low level of water might contribute to early liner failure or unfavorable conditions for your plants. If your pond has a pump and the level falls below the intake, the motor will burn out. In hot weather, evaporation can lower the level rapidly. To avoid shock to fish or growth of algae, replacement water should be added gradually over a period of several days.

To avoid decaying leaf problems in your pond, a hand-held skimmer should be used to remove fallen leaves. If leaf accumulation is heavy, the pond can be covered with a screen or net.

As in other gardens, you hope that your plants will thrive and grow. To prevent overcrowding, start new plants and maintain healthy plants by dividing plants when needed. Generally, lift and divide marginals every two to three years and lilies every three to four years. Because each plant species has special requirements, it is best to check with your local supplier for proper care.

To keep foliage healthy looking, remove faded flowers or yellow leaves once a week. Water lilies and other decorative plants will benefit from fertilization every 30 days. Pelletized fertilizer is pushed into the soil at the base of each plant. Once the growing season has ended, fertilization is no longer necessary.

Pond liners and fiberglass shells are not fragile but are prone to leaks. Patching kits are available from your local supplier. Remove the object causing the leak and patch according to kit instructions.

Still water in a pond can become a breeding area for mosquitos. To avoid problems with mosquitos and other insects, install waterfalls and fountains to circulate water. Additional control can be gained by stocking the pond with fish. Insecticides should be avoided.

Winterizing water gardens

If your pond is located in a cold climate, it will need to be "closed" for the winter. Remove the filter after the first frost and allow foliage to die naturally. Once the marginals' aquatic foliage has turned brown, they can be reduced in height by approximately $2/3$. Hardy water lilies should be moved to a deeper section of the pond for the winter. Sensitive plants might need to be stored in indoor ponds for the winter. Plants will survive as long as the water does not freeze to the rootstock. Installation of a heater in northern climates will prevent total freezing.

Most fish can be left in the pond year-round as long as ice does not cover the entire surface for more than a week or two. If your pond is stocked with fancy or tropical varieties of fish, they should be overwintered indoors in a cold-water aquarium.

9

Arbors, trellises, and garden structures

Arbors and trellises are features that are usually identified with old English gardens. They provide shade-enclosed walkways for the pleasure of participants in outdoor living spaces. Today, they serve much the same purpose, acting as pleasant transitions from one area to another in your garden. Typically, these features are structures that support plant material overhead. They might, however also function as green screens or living walls (FIG. 9-1).

Garden structures

Garden structures are useful for storing garden tools as well as providing for shelter against sun, wind, or rain. Check local building codes. In most communities, you must obtain a building permit to construct outdoor structures.

When designing the structure, consider sun or wind control along with any plumbing and electrical needs. To increase the usefulness of your deck, patio, or yard, a roofed structure can be considered (FIG. 9-2). A roof can help tie the deck or patio into the architecture of the house and will certainly provide protection from direct sun.

If day-long direct sun is a problem, canvas might be a possible solution. Filtered sun can be provided with the use of louvers or an egg crate design. Other typical coverings that can be used include cedar shakes, asphalt and gravel, corrugated fiberglass panels, screens, and lath. If you will be constructing a roof structure, a head clearance of 7 to 8 feet is usu-

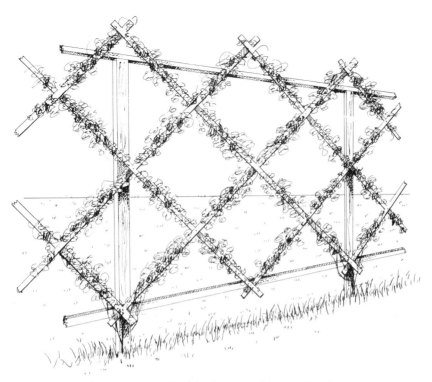

Fig. 9-1. *A light frame covered with vines provides an airy fence.*

ally sufficient. If the roof is to be watertight, it needs to be pitched to allow for runoff.

Garden structures share similar elements as those found in deck construction. Many structures are post and beam design. Posts are set in the ground securely and support horizontal beams that support roof rafters set at right angles to the beams. A ledger along the house acts as support for the opposite end of the rafters. Posts 4×4 inches are usually considered sufficient for most garden structures. Posts can be anchored several ways:

- Directly in the ground with soil firmly tamped around the base. They should be set at least 3 feet below grade.
- In unstable soil, concrete should be added to the hole for firmer support.
- Posts can be permanently anchored to concrete piers using pre-manufactured metal anchors.
- Premanufactured metal anchors can be used to secure posts to existing concrete slabs.

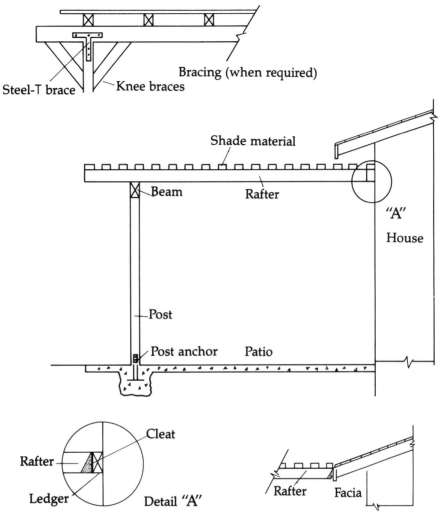

Steel-T brace   Knee braces   Bracing (when required)

Shade material

Beam   Rafter

"A"

House

Post

Post anchor   Patio

Cleat

Rafter

Ledger   Detail "A"

Rafter   Facia

Fig. 9-2. Typical detail of shade structure.

Construction

This section covers several basic steps used in the construction of a shade structure for your garden. First, lay out the location of all posts carefully. Cut posts to the proper length. Set the posts by one of the methods discussed previously, making sure they are secured firmly.

Cut the ledger to length and attach it to the wall. If the structure is free-standing, beams will be on another set of posts and no ledger will be required.

Cut rafters to length and do any decorative scroll work while the boards are still on the ground. Place the rafters on the beam and ledger.

The rafters can be set on top of the ledger or hung in premanufactured hangers. Toenail the boards in place, checking the spacing between rafters. A rule of thumb suggests that the span of a beam is determined by its size. Therefore, a 2-×-6 beam should be supported by posts a maximum of 6 feet apart, while a 2-×-8 beam can have posts 8 feet apart. Rafters are oftentimes spaced on 24-inch centers with a 2-×-6 span up to 10 feet between ledger and beam. Twelve-foot spans need 2-×-8 rafters and 16-foot spans need 2-×-10 rafters.

Check to see that the structure is standing plumb and make any adjustments if necessary. To prevent racking or swaying in the future, gussets or corner braces are added. These braces are diagonal pieces attached in the corners from a post to a rafter. If the rafters are not installed in a design that is the finished covering, installing the chosen covering is the final step (FIG. 9-3).

Fig. 9-3. Pleasant environments are created with a shade structure.

Arbors and trellises

Trellises are thought by many to be one of the earliest known types of garden fencing. Original construction consisted of weaving together light, flexible branches, such as bamboo. Today, a trellis can be regarded as an ornamental fence or screen constructed of light wood strips that cross each other, forming a regular pattern of open spaces, which may or may not support vines or other plants (FIG. 9-4).

The choice of trellis size and design plus the plants that adorn them will be dictated by the site and desired effect. A front door, service entry, or garage front are areas that could all benefit from a trellis structure. Obviously, these sites are all quite diverse and will require different treatments.

You might want to add a touch of privacy with the use of a trellis as a fence screen or by adding a trellis cap to an existing fence or wall. Entryways into gardens are often softened and highlighted with the use of a trellis arbor. An arbor is a three-dimensional extension of a trellis that creates a secluded and enclosed area. The arbor is constructed of similar sections of trellis that are connected together to frame a patio area or pathway (FIG. 9-5). The design chosen should be kept open and simple so as to complement surrounding architectural features, not compete for attention.

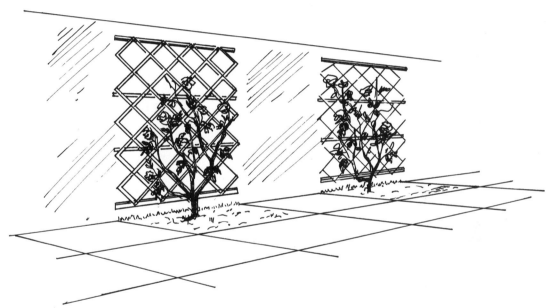

Fig. 9-4. *A trellis for training special plants.*

In the world of children, a trellis or arbor provides the temptation to climb. While you might be able to police this climbing activity, there will be times when this becomes impossible. To avoid possible injuries, build a strong trellis and protect it with a thorny plant such as a climbing rose. Because children are not the only people that might climb your "garden ladder," locate your trellis so that it will not provide an easy access to your home. Again, thorny plants growing throughout the trellis will deter much of this unwanted climbing.

Trellises are quite a simple do-it-yourself garden construction project. In our society of premade everything (or so it seems at times), trellises can be made using preconstructed lath panels. These panels are sold in units 4-feet wide and 8-feet long and are usually pressure-treated or of a wood type, such as redwood or cedar, that is decay-resistant. Because of their uniformity, however, creativity is limited. If you will be using lath panels, follow these simple steps to ensure success.

Dig post holes 18 to 24 inches deep. Use a string line to keep the holes aligned and to mark spacing easily ahead of time. If your posts are not purchased with a decorative top, but you want to have "something," it is best to do this before installing the posts.

Set posts in holes using another string line as a guide for uniform height. Pour concrete in post holes. Using temporary braces, secure posts to maintain alignment and plumb. Allow concrete to cure for two to three days.

Cut sections of 2×4 to fit between the posts, both top and bottom. These boards can be secured to the center of each post by hanging them in premanufactured metal hangers or toenailing.

Cut a section of lath to fit between the posts. To get the most economical use out of the panels, make pieces 2 feet wide or the full 4-foot width. Secure the panel using galvanized fasteners to both top and bottom cross pieces.

To cover free ends of the lath panel, 1-×-1-inch trim can be used to box in the panel and finish the look. The amount of trim or "gingerbread" you add is entirely up to your imagination and ability.

Commercially made trellises should generally be avoided. Too often, they are constructed of materials too light to provide good support. An additional problem caused by metal and plastic preconstructed trellises is heat accumulation. These materials can get very hot in the sun and retain the heat, which causes serious problems for any vines growing on them.

Knot-free, first-grade lumber should be used for your project. The dimensions of the lumber will depend on the plants you want to support and the style of the finished trellis. Light, airy trellises can be constructed of lath or 1-inch-thick stock. To support wisteria or grapes, 2-inch or greater stock might be required. It is always better to build the trellis a little heavier than necessary. It is very discouraging to have the trellis break just as the vines reach maturity.

Using graph paper, draw an outline of the finished trellis in an appropriate scale. Next, work with different combinations of cross members until you like what you see. Remember, however, that the true beauty of a trellis might be the plants growing on it rather than its architecture. Transfer the measurements from your graph paper to your wood

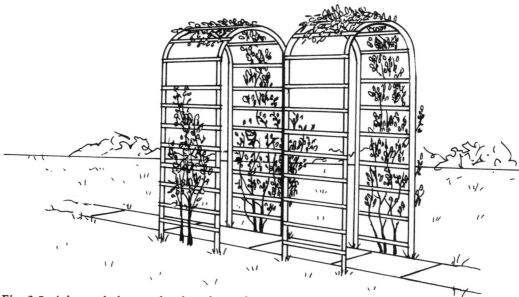

Fig. 9-5. Arbor and plant-enclosed garden path.

stock, taking the time to be accurate. Fasten the pieces together, holding them securely using galvanized fastening hardware (FIG. 9-6).

Setting the posts

The support of the structure is achieved with a ground stake or post. Posts anchored in concrete offer the best support. Dig the post holes 18 to 24 inches deep. In areas where frost upheaval is a problem, the hole needs to be sufficiently deep enough to anchor the post below the frost-line. Place 2 to 4 inches of coarse gravel in the bottom of each hole, setting the posts on this base. Provide temporary support to keep the post plumb while concrete is added and allowed to cure. Detailed directions for handling concrete can be found in chapter 3 on patios. After the concrete has cured, the temporary supports can be removed and the assembled trellis panels attached to the posts.

The trellis should be constructed either of wood that is decay-resistant or treated to prevent decay. The preservative material used is important because the soil around the trellis will be used for planting. Creosote is one such product that is a good preservative but it also can contaminate the soil. Some paints might cause a similar problem.

If you chose to paint, you also need to consider the color carefully. The color of the house, its trim color, and any color added by flowers or foliage all add to the difficult choice of choosing a color. White is not an imaginative color, but it is safe choice, blending with every other color. If

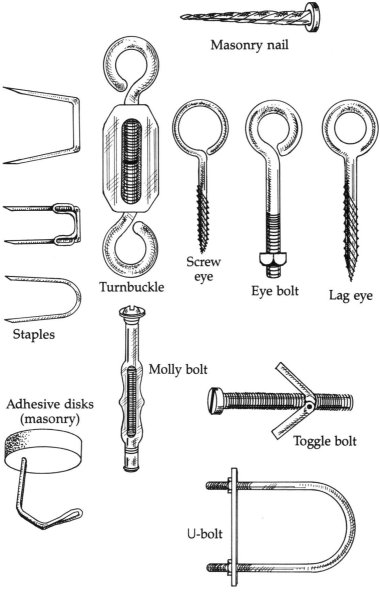

Masonry nail

Turnbuckle

Screw
eye

Eye bolt

Lag eye

Staples

Molly bolt

Adhesive disks
(masonry)

Toggle bolt

U-bolt

Fig. 9-6. Standard fastening hardware for arbors and trellises.

you paint the trellis the same color as your house, it will seem to disappear into the wall, allowing the vines to create a pattern of foliage and flowers against the wall.

Whatever color you choose, take the time to paint your trellis correctly. Prepare the wood with a primer/sealer coat and at least two finished coats of color. The primer coat and the first color coat can be applied before pieces are assembled. After assembly, the final coat of paint will ensure complete coverage and protection for your trellis.

Foliage

Planting your favorite vine or shrub is the final step in adding a trellis or arbor to your garden. Roses and grapes are probably the plants that come to mind first for many people (FIG. 9-7). These are only the tip of the iceberg of plant choices.

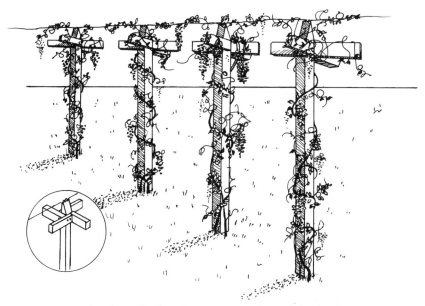

Fig. 9-7. *A simple trellis for vine support and vivid displays.*

Clematis is a perennial vine that is an airy, lightweight plant covered with an abundance of flowers. To get the show of color from clematis, the root zone should be shaded during the hot days of summer with low shrubs or other perennial plantings. The choice of color, bloom size, and season of bloom, is probably greater in this group of plants than any others. Some varieties of clematis also offer a seed head that will add additional interest to your garden in yet another season. Your local nursery/garden center will be able to suggest varieties that are hearty in your area.

Akebia provides an interesting chocolate-colored flower in the spring. Silver lace-vine, also known as Chinese fleece-vine, is a good perennial choice for a fast-growing climber. Bittersweet vine provides a bonus in the fall with its masses of orange-colored pods. Pruning this plant in the fall will allow you to take advantage of these pods in indoor bouquets and arrangements.

Ivy is often used to provide a green, leafy wall. A rough-textured wood trellis will most benefit this plant, providing more "foot holds" for the climbing rootlets to attach. Ivy can get very aggressive and should be used sparingly and tended regularly. An old garden friend once explained the frustration with ivy the following way: The first year after planting, ivy sleeps. The second year it creeps. The third year it leaps. Be prepared to control that leap.

A final perennial suggestion that requires little care is the sweet pea. The shoots die back each year but the root stock survives, sending out vines that produce pink, red, or white flowers over a long season.

Annual vines are an excellent choice for variety and easy care of a trellis (FIG. 9-7). Because these vines do not remain all year, the trellis does not get overcrowded and maintenance and repairs are more easily performed (FIG. 9-8).

Fig. 9-8. A trellis panel helps define and enclose a deck area.

Two favorite annual vines that deserve consideration are the morning glory and moonflower. Morning glories are available in blue, white, blue with a white star throat, and red. The moonflower, like the morning glory, has the ability to grow rapidly and cover large areas. It differs in that the plants are nocturnal, with the white blossoms opening in early evening. If that's not enough reason to consider this plant, you should also know that it has a very pleasant scent that enhances your enjoyment of a quiet evening garden. Figure 9-9 offers a few additional annual vine selections.

Annual Vines

Common Name	Botanical Name	Typical Size	Plant Characteristics	Color of Bloom
Balloon-vine	Cardispernum halicacabum	10'-15'	Full sun, good soil.	White
Canary-bird vine	Tropaeolum pergrinum	10'-18'	Shady, Moist soil.	Canary yellow
Gourd vine	Lagenaria vulgaris (large) Cucubita pepo ovifera (small)	8'-20'	Full sun, good soil, not particular.	Assorted fruits
Morning glory Heavenly blue Pearly gate Blue star Scarlett O'Hara Darling	Ipomoea purpurea	10'-15'	Any good soil, full sun..	Blue White Pale blue Red Wine red
Moonflower	Calonyction aculeatum	10'-20'	Same as for morning glory. Nocturnal.	White
Sweet pea	Lathyrus odoratus	4'-8'	Early planting, cool climate best.	Various

Fig. 9-9. Some annual vine favorites.

10

Lighting

Lighting is the finishing touch to any garden. Not only should lighting be considered to enhance your nighttime enjoyment of your garden, it also enhances safety. Contrary to popular belief, lighting can be an economical addition to your garden. With today's wide range of selections, you need not be an electrician to install low-voltage lighting systems.

A garden lit at night has a touch of magic and mystique. Good lighting emphasizes a garden's best features while allowing the rest to remain in darkness. Garden lighting is a wise investment, making a small garden seem spacious or a large estate intimate.

Throughout history, outdoor lighting has played an important role in safety and worship (for example, Japanese lanterns at walkways and temples). With recent developments and advances in lighting, garden lighting has become sophisticated, yet it is still simple enough to understand and install for the do-it-yourselfer.

If your lighting needs require the use of a 120-volt power source, you'll not only need an electrical permit, but probably the services of a qualified electrician as well. In fact, most communities will require this. A 120-volt power source is usually only needed for intense nighttime lighting, such as to enjoy your favorite sport (basketball, tennis, and such), add extra security, or to illuminate parking areas and swimming pools. The services of a qualified electrician are most needed in swimming pool areas, where the need exists for wiring underwater lighting as well as area lighting. Regardless of whether you do the work yourself or hire someone to do it, it is important to learn as much about lighting as possible. The information that follows is intended to highlight some important features of lighting and then guide you through designing and installing your own system.

Types of lighting

The reasons you choose to light are as varied as the techniques employed to accomplish your results. Techniques, in general, vary in the location of the light source and the direction the light is aimed; up, down, or across a surface.

Down lighting

Down lighting refers specifically to any type of lighting that is projected from above an object. Generally, a floodlight is used to illuminate a large area for safety, security, or entertainment. In some cases, one or more floodlights might be used to emphasize a special plant or object in your garden. Properly installed, down lighting mimics natural lighting produced by the sun and moon.

Up lighting

Up lighting, in contrast to down lighting, is produced by placing the light source below an object or area. Up lighting adds dramatic impact to a garden by demanding a viewer's attention. Lighting such as this rarely occurs in nature and must be added to any garden with a stroke of discretion.

Safety lighting

Considered to be one of the most important functions of garden lighting, safety lighting allows you to enjoy your garden at night. Properly installed safety lighting permits easy movement and more comfortable use of your outdoor rooms. Safety lighting is typically used along driveways, walkways, and changes in elevation at steps.

Security lighting

Security lighting might light the same areas as safety lighting but it is intended to protect yards from unwelcome guests. Protection is provided through the even distribution of illumination, leaving no pockets of dark as potential hideaways. A glaring and offensive system is not needed. To be totally effective, the system must be easily operated. Proper switches will allow you to operate all or just parts of the system as needed.

Area lighting

Area lighting is used to illuminate a deck or play area without producing glare in the area or for your neighbors. A combination of floodlights placed high and decorative lights appropriately placed will provide ample, nonglaring light. Globes or panels are often used in dining areas to soften and diffuse light sources.

Moon lighting

Moon lighting is a technique that can easily create the feeling of a moon-lit night every night. Several mild intensity lights placed high into trees or on buildings will help create this very natural and relaxing effect. Best results are obtained when the light source is both very high and hidden.

Solar-powered lighting

Many companies have solar-powered lights available. These lights have a photocell collector that gathers sunlight during the day. The light unit stores this energy for use after sunset. The style most commonly available is the mushroom-type or pagoda light. Because the collector cells are typically small in size, the amount of stored energy is small, limiting the light intensity and duration. Another solar powered novelty available is a lighted house number sign.

The advantage of solar-powered units is the ability to install them quickly without extensive wiring. Consider the area for placement carefully, most of the collector cells are permanently attached to the light. Ask your dealer if any units are available with a portable collector cell. This type of unit will allow you to place the light in a more recessed shady area, and the collector in a fully sunny area.

These are but a few of the many lighting techniques available to the designer. Other techniques include spotlighting, silhouetting, perspective lighting, and water-feature lighting. Most lighting supply stores have representatives that can discuss the best methods to solve your particular goals.

Many of these techniques can best be accomplished through use of standard 120-volt lighting systems. New materials and lights are available in 12-volt systems that can extend the range of possibilities for your garden. It is no longer necessary to be a licensed electrician to install your own lighting. A combination of 120-volt and 12-volt lighting systems is most common in the home garden. You probably already have a 120-volt system to provide security and safety lighting. Supplementing this with a 12-volt system provides a complete lighting package.

If you are doing new work or remodeling, it is important to review

	12 Volt	120 Volt
1) Safety - Installation	simple and safe to install	usually requires permits and the assistance of a licensed electrician
2) Brightness	usually range from dim to medium bright - takes more lights per area for bright light	range of brightness from dim to brilliant - some lamps are capable of lighting several thousand square feet
3) Installation Cost	relatively inexpensive	more expensive, up to twice as much as a 12 volt system if you do it yourself, even more if an electrician is hired
4) Maintenance	need annual lubrication of lamp sockets, cleaning debris from uplights, recheck direction of light beam.	same as 12 volt
5) Durability	range from poor to excellent depending on the materials, maintenance, and exposure - the better the quality, the longer it will last	same as 12 volt
6) Relocation	very easy to relocate	since 120 volt systems are more permanently installed (conduit in most cases) relocation is more involved
7) Best Application	best in small gardens or intimate areas of larger gardens	useful in areas where brilliant illumination may be required for safety, security, or recreation - brighter lamps make lighting of huge trees more effective

Fig. 10-1. *Comparison of a 12-volt lighting system and a 120-volt lighting system.*

the pros and cons of 120-volt (standard voltage) and 12-volt (low voltage) system (FIG. 10-1).

Lighting terminology

The terms *lamp* and *light bulb* are interchangeable and refer to the part of the lighting system that emits the light. There are many different types of lamps yielding many different types of light. Probably the most common lamp is the incandescent. Other lamps include quartz incandescent, fluorescent, mercury vapor, and high-pressure sodium. No matter which type of lamp you choose to go with, it is best to remain with primarily one type of lighting. The following points should be considered carefully before purchasing lamps:

- Efficiency. Efficiency, measured in lumens per watt of electrical input, refers to the amount of light output for a particular lamp. A typical example is the 65-watt light bulb that yields the same illumination as a less-efficient, standard 75-watt light bulb.

- Lamp Size. Lamp size and light output indicate how bright the lighting system is. Watts of electricity consumed is the rate used to size lamps. Using the previous example, the wattage consumed is 65, while the output is equivalent to a standard 75-watt bulb.

- Color emission. Color emission refers to the characteristic color generated by a particular lamp. Mercury vapor lamps have a characteristic blue color. Color can be used as part of your plan, but it is important to be aware of not only the positive but the negative effects it might have on your garden.

- Lamp life. Lamp life is usually measured by the number of hours it will burn light. The longer a lamp yields light, the less frequently it will need to be replaced, an important consideration for hard-to-reach fixtures.

- Cost. Cost is always important. A wide range exists between the smallest incandescent lamp and a high-intensity lamp. The lamp size, efficiency, and life all determine the cost. Usually, the more expensive high-energy lamps are more cost-effective than less-expensive incandescent lamps.

Fixtures

The unit that houses a lamp is the light fixture. Here, as with other component parts, the choices of styles and their purposes are almost limitless. Some common choices include bullet lights, well or recessed lights, post lights (ranging from 3 to 8 feet or more), bollard lights (typically 2 to 3 feet in height), porch lights, low-area lights (most commonly known as mushroom or pagoda lamps), and recessed stair lights (set into the sides or risers of steps for accent and safety).

Fixtures and lamps alone do not make a complete lighting system. Additional component parts outlined might be needed as dictated by your power source (120 volt or 12 volt).

Wires

Wires are identified by an industry-wide size and type system. A number is assigned to the size of a wire. The smaller the number, the greater the thickness of the wire. A typical type of wire for outdoor use would be UF (underground feeder). The size of UF wire commonly recommended is 12-2. This designation indicates that the wire is composed of 2 leads or cables, each being #12 in size.

On systems with long runs or that need a greater capacity, #10 is suggested. Burial depths and conduit requirements are specified by local codes for all 120-volt installations. Conduit is any pipe (metal or plastic) that encloses and protects outdoor wiring. The easiest to use and usually least-expensive conduit is PVC (polyvinyl chloride). The expense and need for conduit is usually not required for 12-volt lighting systems.

Junction boxes, switches, and outlets

Connections to light fixtures, switches, and outlets are contained within a box. The boxes (required on all 120-volt systems) provide a safe, weatherproof area for wires to be joined and hidden. The connections made are extremely important because, at the least, the failure of a connection can lead to failure of the system, and potential electrical and fire hazards. Wire nuts, the most common connector, are screwed onto the ends of wires. They not only twist the wire further together, but also act as a "hat," covering and protecting the bare wires.

Turning the system on and off is accomplished through any one of many different switches. The standard toggle switch merely turns the system on and off while a dimmer switch allows you to control the brightness of your system when turned on. Automatic control is achieved with the use of time clocks that will turn the system on and off at preset times. Another common type of automatic switch is a photocell. As the photocell senses less light, for whatever reason, it will turn your system on. It also can sense too much light, turning the system off. For this reason, it is important that the photocell not be located in the direct path of a light just turned on, the system would only continue to cycle on and off.

Transformers

The component items previously mentioned are common to 120-volt and 12-volt lighting systems. Transformers, however, are unique to 12-volt systems only. As the name implies, the unit transforms or changes something. The something in this case is electric voltage. A transformer is either plugged into or wired into a 120-volt power system. This source is then converted into a discharge output of only 12 volts. A low-voltage lighting system must have at least one transformer, and it must be connected at some point to a 120-volt power source. Transformers are available for outside installation—having watertight boxes—and might contain photocells or timers for automatic operation of your lighting system.

Planning your lighting system

In order for your adventure in lighting to be successful, a few design principles should be remembered. Using these points when reviewing your needs or when critiquing an existing system will help avoid problems, errors, and frustrations:

- Study natural light, noting how plants and objects are highlighted. Mimicking the effects of sunlight and moonlight will give your garden a more natural and comfortable feeling.

- Don't overlight. Remember, you are trying to set a mood, not create harshness.

- Plants and materials have a certain degree of reflectiveness, which might help or hinder your theme. Highly reflective surfaces will appear brilliant when lit and absorptive surfaces might require additional lighting just to be noticed.

- Lamps should be limited to one type. The size and use of the lamp will help create interest in your garden, allowing you to illuminate the important focal points or safety hazards.

- Light generated from a hidden source appears more natural. Hiding the source can also minimize glare. Conceal by placing fixtures high, covering the lamp with a diffusing lens or grill, or by illuminating an area by lighting a reflective surface.

- Fixtures should be located so that they do not interfere with walking, mowing, or maintenance. When placed out of the way, they are less likely to create problems. Switches and lighting controls should, unlike fixtures, be located conveniently. This keeps them out of the way but readily accessible.

- Always install and use electrical systems with safety in mind. Check local codes, secure required permits, and hire qualified electricians on 120-volt power systems.

Lighting ideas

The following is a list of lighting ideas that you might find useful in enhancing your garden or making your walkways and patio areas more safe:

- House entries present a warm and inviting welcome to visitors (FIG. 10-2).

- Garage and driveway areas combined with entry lighting provide not only a pleasing view, but safe access to your home.

- Security lighting of secluded, hidden spots sets the mind at ease. Remember, glaring light is not required, just complete coverage.

Fig. 10-2. This entry walkway is made safer with mushroom lights.

- Safety lighting of steps and walkways will make the garden more enjoyable for you and your guests (FIG. 10-3).
- Decks, patios, and porches offer an excellent area to light both for accent (framing views) and enjoyment (dining or reading).
- Lighting in recreational areas can extend games into the evening. To be effective, lighting for sports such as badminton, croquet, and shuffleboard needs to be bright, uniform, and glare-free.
- Water features lit from an outside source or with lights submerged in the water can be spectacular. Special care in wiring around water requires the services of a licensed electrician.
- Shrubs, trees, flowers, and statuary, of course, can be made spectacular through a properly designed and installed lighting system. Unusually branched trees, such as honey locust (Gleditsia triacanthos inermis), white oak (Quercus alba), red oak (Quercus rubra), and southern live oak (Quercus virginiana) can add a spectacular canopy of interest when lit from above. For lower understory trees that can be spot lit, choose trees for their colorful foliage, fruit, or unique flowers. A short list would include blue atlas cedar (Cedrus atlantica "Glauca"), kousa dogwood (Cornus kousa), hawthorns (Crataegus species), and southern magnolia (Magnolia grandifloria).

Fig. 10-3. *Interesting gardens by day are still inviting at night with the use of proper lighting.*

It is important to study plants carefully before selecting the type of lighting. Plants such as ornamental flowering plum (Prunus cerasifera "Thundercloud") and Colorado blue spruce (Picea pungens "Glauca") have unattractive undersides and should only receive down lighting for best effects.

Designing lighting

Now that you know about lamps and fixtures and have a good idea of what and why you are lighting, the fun begins! The step-by-step process in this section will allow you, with your new-gained knowledge, to switch on a new environment.

Make a sketch of your property. Draw all existing features on a piece of graph paper. Locate buildings, walkways, trees, and any other permanent features as accurately as possible and to scale. Any proposed additions to your property should also be added to your drawing (see the example shown in Appendix G).

Wish-list items include all the things you think you would like to accomplish with your lighting system. Add these to a sheet of tracing paper laid overtop of your property sketch. Highlight the areas and features you want to emphasize. Make notes right on the sheet. It is important to know all that you want and why you want or need it.

Set priorities for your lighting. On an additional sheet of tracing paper, mark in the lighting needs of a particular object or area. Indicate the fixture and the lamp that would best satisfy those needs. Once this is all on paper, you can check off the areas that take priority over other areas. If budget is no concern, this list won't even be needed. For those of us who must operate within a budget, however, a complete plan is important so that you will have a unified and comprehensive system.

Installation

Install the entire system, or only a phase, using your design sketch as your blueprint. The first year might see only the installation of the major components as dictated by your design. Each subsequent year will see additional priorities installed until the entire system is complete, providing the mood and environment you designed.

A 12-volt system is easier to install but care must still be exercised. Some 12-volt systems contain instructions for installing their own kit. If it is included, follow the manufacturer's steps, some warranties depend on it. Get any permits required for 120-volt systems or, in some cases, for a low-voltage system.

Maintenance

Periodic maintenance of your system will provide continued enjoyment for many years. Regardless of the power source, some basic maintenance is standard, such as cleaning debris and leaves from around light fixtures. Lamps can be wiped clean but only when cold.

Select durable fixtures near salt-exposed environments to minimize damage due to corrosion. To avoid lamps rusting into fixture sockets, a silicone-based lubricant should be sprayed in the sockets at least once a year.

The final maintenance task really starts before installation with proper fixture location. As your garden matures, plants grow and sometimes crowd light fixtures. Because 12-volt systems usually don't require wires to be trench-buried, they can usually be easily relocated. A light fixture connected to 120-volt power source can be easily relocated a short distance by planning ahead of time.

Additional considerations

The comfort of your outdoor living space might be jeopardized with the invasion of insects. Unfortunately, outdoor lighting will add to the attractiveness of your garden for bugs. Planning for pests can help eliminate a good portion of the problem.

Game and recreation areas that require bright floodlights or spot lights, should be located as far from the entertainment area as possible. Placing lights high will also help, by attracting the insects above your head and away from you.

Selective placement of lights to draw insects away from entertainment areas provides some relief from pests. Because most insects are attracted to blue light, mercury vapor lights in a distant area of your garden will draw insects away from activity areas.

In combination with blue mercury lights, yellow "bug lights" can be installed. These lamps block the blue light and are not "seen" by the insects. These lamps, however, are not very attractive or energy efficient.

Light only the areas of your garden that require it. All lights in the garden need not be lit if you only want to sit and read a book.

A final solution for a heavily infested area is the installation of an insect trap. Many types of insect traps are available that attract either by sight (blue light) or scent (sex pheremones).

Appendix A
Tool checklist

	TOOL	OWN	RENT	BUY
G E N E R A L	claw hammer			
	hand sledge hammer			
	hand saw			
	circular saw with masonry blades			
	tape measure			
	framing square			
	carpenter's level			
	line level			
	10" x 10" hand tamper			
	digging shovel			
	flat shovel			
	rake			
	soft bristle broom			
	hand broom			
	knee pads			
	string line			
	wheelbarrow			
	garden hose			
	safety goggles			
B R I C K	rubber mallet			
	brick chisel			
	brick layer's hammer			
	brick tongs			
C O N C R E T E	concrete mixer			
	mixing hoe			
	mortar board			
	steel float			
	wood float			
	bull float			
	pointed trowel			
	joint tool			

Appendix B
Verifying squareness

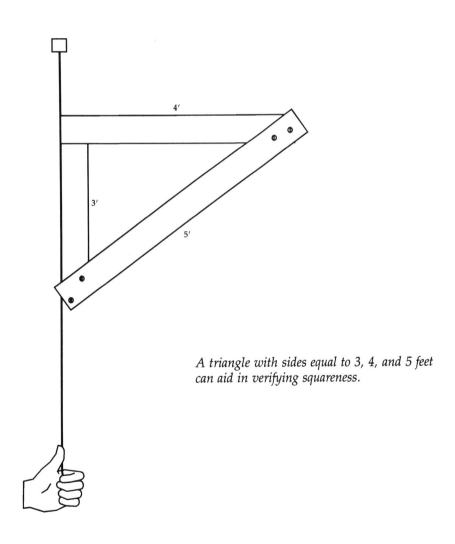

A triangle with sides equal to 3, 4, and 5 feet can aid in verifying squareness.

Appendix C
Fasteners

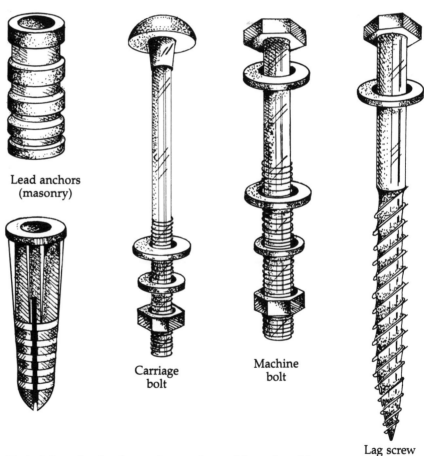

Lead anchors
(masonry)

Carriage
bolt

Machine
bolt

Lag screw

Typical fastening hardware that can be used in various jobs.

Appendix D
Step formulas

Vertical Drop	Number Of Steps	Tread	Span
42"	6	11 1/4"	56 1/4"
36"	5	11 1/4"	45"
30"	4	11 1/4"	33 3/4"
24"	3	11 1/4"	22 1/2"
18"	3	11 1/4"	22 1/2"
12"	2	11 1/4"	11 1/4"

Various deck heights require a different number of steps.

Appendix E
Common weights and measures

Weights

Unit	Abbreviation	Equivalent
ton		2,000 pounds
hundredweight	cwt	100 pounds
pound	lb	16 ounces

Capacity

Unit	Abbreviation	Equivalent
gallon	gal	4 quarts
quart	qt	2 pints

Length

Unit	Abbreviation	Equivalent
mile	mi	5,280 feet, 1,760 yards
yard	yd	3 feet, 36 inches
foot	ft or '	12 inches
inch	in or "	----

Area

Unit	Abbreviation	Equivalent
acre	---	4,840 sq. yds, 43,560 sq. ft.
square yard	sq. yd.	9 sq. ft., 1,296 sq. in.
square foot	sq. ft.	144 square inches
square inch	sq. in.	-----

Volume

Unit	Abbreviation	Equivalent
cubic yard	cu. yd.	27 cu. ft., 46,656 cu. in.
cubic foot	cu. ft.	1,728 cu. in.
cubic inch	cu. in.	------

Appendix F
Formulas

length × width   = area (two-dimensional measurement)
pi × radius squared = area of a circle (pi = 3.14)
$^1/_2$ base × height   = area of a triangle

To arrive at a volume measure, multiply the area times depth or height.

Appendix G
Sample plot plan

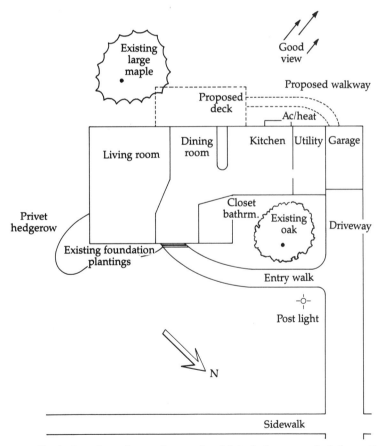

A generalized plot plan of your home should include as much information on your landscape as possible, especially if it pertains directly to your project.

Glossary

aggregate   Crushed stone used for a subbase and in concrete mixes where it is generally divided into larger stones, or coarse aggregate, and sand particles as fine aggregates.

air-dried   Dried by exposure to air without supplemental heat.

backfill   The replacement of excavated soil.

baluster (spindle)   Vertical member in a railing between top rail and bottom rail or stair tread.

batter   Refers to the backward slope of a wall from the base to the cap.

batter board   A goal, postlike structure used to indicate desired heights. String lines attached to these structures are used to frame the outline of a construction project.

beam   Structural member of a deck used to support joists.

butt joint   The point where the ends of two boards meet in a square-cut joint.

canopy layer   An overhead zone of vegetation that functions much the same way as an umbrella (shading outdoor living areas).

caulk   A compound used in waterproofing.

CCA (chromated copper arsenate)   Greenish in color, CCA is the most common chemical preservative used in pressure-treating wood.

counter-boring   The enlargement of a hole for only a portion of its depth to allow the head of a screw or bolt to be flush with the surface.

dead load   The weight of the materials in a structure.

deciduous plants   Plants that shed their leaves each autumn.

decking   The top surface of a deck.

drip lines The outermost edge of the branches in a tree's canopy.

espalier Means to grow plants in a flat plane that may or may not be attached to a surface for support.

fasteners Nails, bolts, screws, lag screws, and other hardware used to secure components of structures.

flagstone Flat stones, usually 1 to 4 inches thick, used as a hard surfacing material for walks, steps, and patios.

flashing Sheet metal or other material used to protect a building from water seepage.

footings Usually made of concrete, footings are designed to support the weight of a deck while holding deck posts in place.

frostline The depth of frost penetration into the soil. Varies in different climates throughout the country.

grain The direction or arrangement of the wood fibers in a board.

grout A material, usually mortar, used to fill joints and cavities between bricks and stones.

heartwood The older, nonfunctioning central core of a tree, often darker in color and more naturally resistant to decay.

joists Structural lumber used to support deck boards.

kiln-dried Wood dried with supplemental heat.

lag screws Large screws with hex heads that can be installed with a wrench or ratchet.

landscape features Walkways, patios, decks, fences, walls, fountains, arbors, statues, and reflecting pools/ponds.

ledger A joist support attached to a house.

level Exactly horizontal.

live load Load imposed on a structure by occupants, furniture, snow, etc.

lumber (dimension) Wood 2 to 5 inches thick and 2 or more inches wide, such as joists and rafters.

lumen The amount of light emitted by a lamp. One lumen is the amount of light emitted by one standard candle.

nails *Common nails* used in most general construction range in size from 2d to 60d. *Boxed nails* have thinner shafts than common nails. Typically, they are used for light construction and range in size from 2d to 40d. *Double-headed nails* are used in any construction that needs to be easily disassembled, such as in bracing and forms. *Masonry nails* might have round, square, or fluted shafts and are designed to be driven into concrete, masonry, or stone.

on center (oc) The measurement of spacing from the center of one piece to the center of another.

pier A column, usually of concrete, used to support posts.

plumb Exactly vertical.

plumb bob A weight suspended on the end of a string used to establish vertical lines in the positioning of posts and stakes.

post A deck member that transfers the weight of a deck to the footings.

pressure-treating A process by which a chemical preservative is forced into lumber under high pressure to make it resistant to rot and insect damage.

reinforcing Metal screen or steel rods placed in concrete to increase strength.

rise The vertical height of an individual step.

saws *Crosscut saws* are used to cut across the grain of the wood. *Ripsaws* are used to cut with the grain of a board.

screed A long, straight board used to level concrete or sand set in forms.

setbacks Distances required between permanent buildings and other buildings or property lines.

silicon caulk One of a group of polymerized organics available as resins, coatings, or sealants providing excellent waterproofing.

span The total horizontal distance from top to bottom of a flight of steps.

stringer Structural lumber used to support treads in constructing stairs.

tread The horizontal board in a stairway on which you step.

UCC (Uniform Construction Codes) Regulations that govern construction at the state and local levels.

Index

About the authors

John D. Webersinn is the owner of Webersinn's Landscaping. Mr. Webersinn has taught horticulture and landscape design both at Shelton College and in local adult community education programs. Mr. Webersinn is the vice president of the Cape May County Board of Agriculture; vice president of the board of managers for the New Jersey Agricultural Experiment Stations/Cook College; chairman for the New Jersey Nursery and Landscape Association, Southern Chapter; and chairman of the local Shade Tree Commission. His degrees include: A.S. (magna cum laude) horticulture and landscape design, Temple University; B.S. St. Mary's College; 40 hours graduate study in mycology and plant protection, Virginia Polytechnic Institute and State University.

Dan Keen, who holds an Associate in Science degree, is a technical writer and computer consultant. Mr. Keen is co-owner, editor, and publisher of a local weekly newspaper. Mr. Keen has written many articles and columns for national computer magazines and trade journals. He has also taught computer science at Stockton State College and in adult community education programs. Mr. Keen is the coauthor of other books published by TAB Books/McGraw-Hill: *Mastering the Tandy 2000, Assembly Language Programming for the TRS-80 Model 16,* and TAB's 49 Science Fair Project Series.